MARRIED TO THE DEMON KING

Married to the Demon King

SUSAN F. KEPNER

SILKWORM BOOKS

ISBN 974-9575-58-x

First published in 2004 by
Silkworm Books
104/5 Chiang Mai–Hot Road, M. 7, Suthep
Chiang Mai 50200, Thailand
Website: www.silkwormbooks.info
E-mail: silkworm@loxinfo.co.th

Set in 12 pt. Adobe Garamond by Silk Type

Printed in Thailand by O. S. Printing House, Bangkok

1 3 5 7 9 10 8 6 4 2

Contents

CONTENTS

Chapter 4
Humor, Myth, and the Prophetic Pen 109

Bibliography *127*

Preface

This is a book about love and marriage in contemporary
Thailand. It is built around six short stories written by "Sri
Daoruang," the pen name of Wanna Sawatsri, a seriously
funny woman who is one of Thailand's leading fiction
writers.

Sri Daoruang called these stories "tales of the demon
folk" (*Rueang chao yak*/เรื่องชาวยักษ์). She took her characters
from the *Ramakian*, the Thai version of the *Ramayana*,
the great Indian epic that made its way into Southeast Asia
centuries ago and was adopted by people from Java to
Cambodia to Siam, all of whom modified it and made it
their own. It is the story of Prince Ram (Rama, in the
original Indian version) and his beloved Princess Sida
(Sita), who is stolen away by the lovesick king of the
demons, Thotsakan (Ravanna). After many thrilling and
romantic adventures, Prince Ram, aided by his brother,
Prince Lak, and Hanuman, the monkey king, rescue
Princess Sida from Lanka, Thotsakan's kingdom.

Sri Daoruang took the unprecedented step of dropping these familiar characters into contemporary Bangkok. Through their adventures, she was able to express her thoughts and feelings about the relations between men and women in contemporary Thai society—cloaked in the comforting garment of myth, and laced with the kind of humor that Thai readers appreciate most, on the evidence of the most widely read modern fiction: ironic, frequently sarcastic, earthy, and ultimately compassionate. She found a way to address the concerns, fears, and hopes of many women without ever identifying herself as a *feminit*—a term borrowed from English, and suggesting large foreign women with no charm and unseemly aspirations.

The difference between *femi-nit* and "femi-nine" is a crucial one. Thai women can and do occupy seats in Parliament, manage banks, practice medicine and law, and arguably comprise the backbone of Thai academia. They ordinarily manage family finances, and the family itself. And yet, Thai society in general continues to reserve its highest praise for women who achieve and maintain a pleasing appearance and manner, in addition to being well educated and competent in their job.

Sri Daoruang views her society from the perspective of an "inside outsider." She is neither *femi-nit*, nor particularly "femi-nine." She grew up very poor, in a rural area, and has only four years of formal education. She is famously reclusive, describes herself as "a housewife who writes stories," and spends her spare time toiling in the vast gardens that she has created surrounding her modest home near Bangkok. She is a keen observer of humanity, a born writer, and a natural humorist. She is also the most original contemporary writer in Thailand.

Chapter 1, "A Writer's Life," presents a brief biographical sketch of Sri Daoruang and of her place in the contemporary Thai literary scene.

Chapter 2, "From *Ramayana* to *Ramakian* to Tales of the Demon Folk," gives an overview of the place of the *Ramakian* in Thai cultural and literary history, and explains story elements and characters in the *Ramakian* that will enable the reader to appreciate both the classic underpinnings of Sri Daoruang's short stories, and the kinds of revisions she has made.

Chapter 3 presents the six "Tales of the Demon Folk":

    Thotsakan and Sida

    Thotsakan Puts Down the Chingchoks

    Thotsakan to the Garden

    Thotsakan: Sick of War

    Sida Puts Out the Fire

    Phaya Khon Possessed

Chapter 4, "Humor, Myth, and the Prophetic Pen," addresses the uses of humor and myth in women's writing in general, and examines Sri Daoruang's tales of the demon folk in particular as "feminist writing in the Thai context."

Unless otherwise noted, all translations from Thai texts are my own.

Transliteration of Thai Terms

Thai names and terms have generally been romanized according to the Royal Institute system. In many cases the original Thai is also provided, either in the text or notes. Below is a guide to the Royal Institute transliteration system.

Vowel	Rhymes with vowel in:
a	across; father
ae	hat
e	hen; hay
i	hit; he
o	hope; or sauce
oe	her (without the "r" sound)
u	too
ue	"u" said with a wide smile

Although each Thai vowel has a short and a long form, this feature has no counterpart in English and is generally not identified in the romanization.

Consonants are rendered as follows. All other consonants are pronounced as in English.

Consonant	Sounds like:
ch	jar, or chin
p	p + b (top boy)
ph	pen
k	go
kh	king
t	t + d (hot dog)
th	ten
ng	sing*
r	trilled "r" sound

*Note: "ng" is also used to begin words, and is considered to be a single consonant.

CHAPTER ONE

Sri Daoruang: A Writer's Life

EARLY LIFE

"Sri Daoruang" is the pen name of Wanna Thappananon Sawatsri, who was born in 1943 in a small town in Phitsanuloke province, the third of eight children.[1] Her father was a railroad worker, her mother sold sweets along the railroad line. Wanna tried to help her mother, running alongside passenger cars. She recalls this first job. "I was running along, yelling *'Khanom cha! Khanom cha!'* ["Sweets for sale!"]—but I was too shy to yell loud enough to sell any!" (Wan Pen 1993: 265) Both parents loved to read,

1. Biographical information on Sri Daoruang has been taken largely from her introductions to her collections of short stories; from Wan Pen 1993, from Anderson 1985, and from her letters to this author. Beyond this chapter, I shall refer to her by her pen name only. Thai writers generally refer to themselves by their pen name in all situations having to do with their writing. Even her husband refers to her as "Sri Daoruang" when speaking of her as a writer.

I

and valued old books, but there was little money for such luxuries. She went to school wearing a *phathung* (wrap-around length of cloth) given to her by a family friend; her formal education ended with the fourth grade. When she was twelve, a woman came to the village looking for children to go to work in Bangkok. Wanna's mother sent her away, despite her pleas to be allowed to return to school. She felt betrayed—and betrayed again when her mother refused a local teacher's offer to raise and educate her. These memories rankled for years. When she was fifteen, her father, in agony with stomach cancer, committed suicide, an act that her mother saw as cowardly abandonment. A few years later, her mother died of tuberculosis. (Wan Pen 1993: 265)

In Bangkok, Wanna worked in several factories, and occasionally as a household maid. At the same time, she enrolled in various courses, studying whatever cost least to learn and promised a future: typing, sewing, even driving, although she had no access to a car. While working in a glass factory, she was appalled to see workers splashed with bits of molten glass. "They would be screaming, and people would be trying to get the buttons of their shirt open, but the glass had already burned into their flesh." (Wan Pen 1993: 267) These memories would eventually result in her first published short story, "One Drop of Glass."

Despite all, Wanna felt that working in the factories, which allowed the freedom of living with five or six friends in a tiny room and bathing in a ditch behind the building, was preferable to working as a maid. She never forgot working for a foreign (Western) family, caring for their children. "One day the man was peeling an apple, and then he handed me the peel to throw away. I felt so demeaned. It was worse, somehow, to be treated that way by a foreigner." (Wan Pen 1993: 268)

In 1959, when she was sixteen years old, Wanna submitted a short story to a magazine in Phitsanuloke. She received an acknowledgment that her story had been received, but nothing further. She interpreted this de facto rejection as proof that she could never be a real writer, and although she continued to write stories, it would be sixteen years before she submitted more of her work for publication.

BECOMING "SRI DAORUANG"

In 1973, Wanna attended a meeting in a factory where she was working. At this meeting, Suchat Sawatsri, a well-known young writer, editor, and political activist, spoke to the workers about the democratic process. Wanna writes:

> In those days, professors and journalists went around to the factories, teaching workers. They would ask if you liked to read, and if you said you did, then they would give you books. When Khun Suchat talked, he talked— you know—like a person who reads books, not like ordinary people talk. But he sat right down on the cement floor with everybody. What did I think of him? I thought he was strange. (Wan Pen 1993: 268)

3

Wanna and Suchat began to see each other, and a few years later, they married.

> When I first knew him, he was amazed at how fast I could read. And then, when I wrote something and showed it to him, he was surprised that someone who had only finished *prathom* 4 [primary grade 4] could write without making a lot of mistakes . . . He told me to write exactly the things that had happened in my life, things that I had seen myself; and later on, when I had more experience, then it would be time to start using my imagination. (268)

Suchat suggested that Wanna take the pen name "Sri Daoruang," which may be translated approximately as "splendid marigold," suggesting both her humble origins and the beauty of her art. In 1975, he published "One Drop of Glass" in *The Social Science Review*, a popular political and literary magazine of which he was then editor in chief.

When her stories were first published, no one knew the identity of "Sri Daoruang." The initial purpose of her "reclusive" behavior was to avoid charges that Suchat was publishing her stories because of their relationship rather than the quality of her work. Neither of them anticipated the later, groundless gossip to the effect that Suchat must have written the stories for her, because she had so little formal education.

Since 1975, Sri Daoruang has written several short novels and over one hundred short stories. She was awarded the PEN Thailand Award in 1978, for "The

Grass Cutter," in 1979 for "The Silence That Begins," and in 1986 for "Mating Snakes." In 1978 she was awarded the Cho Karaket Prize for "It Comes With Voting." In 1984, the collection of short stories entitled *One Drop of Glass* was among five finalists for the SEAWrite Award, the most prestigious Thai literary award; again, in 1986, a collection of her stories, *Matsi* (มัทรี), was a finalist.

Sri Daoruang has one son, Mon, now in his twenties, who also is a writer, and an artist. They live in a small community near Bangkok. Mon was born with multiple heart defects, a fact that has been central to the life of the family. When Mon was a boy, Sri Daoruang wrote a lengthy, touching short story about him entitled "Tanu" (ตาหนู); his illness also appears in one of the tales of the demon folk, "Thotsakan Puts Down the *Chingchoks*."[2]

Sri Daoruang's introductions to her short story collections are at once unusually revealing, and perplexing. Described as "reclusive" by other writers and members of the literary community, she has often referred to herself as "just a housewife who steals time from other tasks in which to write," as in her introduction to the 1990 second printing of the collection *Phap luang ta* (ภาพลวงตา), a title which may be translated as "pictures that fool the eye," or more figuratively, as "illusions," which is probably a better translation of her meaning. She likes to make a point of the fact that she is not "one of the intellectuals," but a housewife (*maeban*/แม่บ้าน) who writes "only what I know"

---

2. I have translated the story "Tanu," but it is unpublished as of this writing.

in time taken from household responsibilities and from her beloved garden. Do the constant references to her housewifely status comprise a defense against being snubbed? Does she feel real contempt for "intellectuals?"[3] Thai society places great importance on diplomas, academic titles, high-level contacts, money, and social position. She has little of any of these.

By and large, I believe that Sri Daoruang ought to be taken at her own evaluation: she is, after all, a housewife, and she is a writer, and she does love her garden. I believe that her protestations of humility are quite genuine, as evidenced in particular by the short story, "The Letter You Never Received," written in the form of a letter to the famous and beloved writer Suwanee Sukhontha, whose tragic death occurred on the date that appears at the head of the letter: 13 February 1984 (B.E. 2527).

Suwanee Sukhontha was the founder and chief editor of *Lalana*, perhaps the first magazine in modern times founded with the intention of publishing articles and fiction that would address (among other things) serious issues in women's lives. Suwanee published several of Sri Daoruang's short stories; yet, because of the latter's shyness, the two never met. "The Letter You Never Received"

3. In 1993, in response to my query about the role of popular Buddhism in her work, her reply consisted of one, uncharacteristically testy sentence in an otherwise warm and cheerful letter: "That's the kind of thing you should ask the intellectuals." At the time, I did not know that a storm had recently ensued over her short story "Matsi," which critics construed as an attack on Buddhism.

is a surprisingly unselfconscious display of humility, shyness, "heroine worship," enormous respect for the distant Khun Suwanee's knowledge, and regret at her own lack of education. Yet, Sri Daoruang's pride in her own identity is revealed just as strongly. In this most unabashedly autobiographical short story, she speaks to Suwanee:

> Please believe that there are many things I want to talk about with you. Not once have I been brave enough. Yet, I was always certain in my heart that the day would come when we would meet, and be friends. However, I'm no good at talking, and as for education, you could say that I have hardly any at all. I have always thought that if I could be friends with someone like you, surely I would glean a few things . . .
>
> Although I was born . . . a long way from your neighborhood in the provincial capital, I used to help some people who had a curry stand, during the big wat fair every year. You and I might have gotten to know each other right there, in front of the wat. We may well have walked right by each other, you and me. You and your children may have sat down and eaten curry at that very stand. Who knows? I might have been the person who spooned it onto your plates, unbeknown to either of us. Never, never guessing that some day I would be sending my short stories to Khun! (Sri Daoruang, "The Letter You Never Received," in *Matsi* 1990, 19–20; my English translation of this story appears in *Two Lines/Tracks*, Olivia Sears, ed. Stanford University, Spring 1995)

In Sri Daoruang's introductions to the collections of her short stories, she swings from humility to defensiveness, from frustration to expressions of joy and wonder: humility and defensiveness when she ponders the limits of her formal education; frustration, when she considers the likelihood that "I probably will never know much . . . "; joy, at the swift, occasional recognition that her life, all in all, has been full of wonders.

> In certain moods, I feel tremendous frustration and sadness that I shall go to the end of my life without having had the opportunity to study and learn—anything! But in other moods, I reflect that I have done and have learned so many exciting things. And happiness—I have known happiness all my life (when I have agreed to be content). And, when the latter mood [comes upon me], then the former feelings of frustration fade." (Introduction to the collection *Phap luang ta,* 1990)

Sometimes, she sets aside defensiveness in favor of pure defense—defense of the "wholly" experienced life, as opposed to the life that is given over entirely to writing, and the "life of the mind." Sri Daoruang, like Sida in her tales of the demon folk, is devoted to gardening, an activity to which she accords (at least) as much value as fiction writing. These are the closing words to the 1993 introduction to the collection *Mae Salu* (Mother Salu/แม่สาลู):[4]

4. The title of this story refers to the name a little boy has given to his favorite blanket.

Once, I was proudly pointing out to the person standing beside me, "Look at that tree—it is a tree that I planted myself, and now, look! How lovely and cheering a sight it is." He responded to my joyful words with the remark that it seemed he had [finally] lost a short story writer to a tree.

I did not [try to] explain anything . . . I was, at that moment, in a mood—and, truly, in another world. A world in which one need never compete with anyone. Any new work of mine . . . whenever it may appear, will explain the relationship between the world of writing, and that other world . . . (Introduction to *Mae Salu*, 1993)

I am aware that these quotations may convey a "crabby" image of the writer that will not prepare the reader for the sense of humor that permeates her work. She can appear, within the few pages of one story, at once sentimental, angry, ruthlessly down-to-earth, "crabby," and very funny. In other words, she seems very like her more-or-less fictional Sida.

It has not been the fashion, of late, to look closely into a writer's life for clues to the "meaning" of his or her work. But I believe that the information about this writer's life which is available to us is a gift that ought not to be refused, for to read the tales of the demon folk without knowing anything about Sri Daoruang's life is to miss so much that matters.

AMONG WRITERS

Sri Daoruang's life and work are a testament to Catherine R. Stimpson's observation that "The combination of being intellectually talented but institutionally marginal is one characteristic of the history of women, education, and literary studies." (Stimpson, "Feminist Criticism," in Greenblatt and Gunn 1992: 254) She is, in certain respects, very much "inside" the Thai literary establishment; but in others, she is irremediably "outside." Her age, her marriage to Suchat Sawatsri, and her associations place her squarely in the midst of the generation of liberal, "leftist" idealists who began their writing careers during the early 1970s, including such highly regarded fiction writers as Khamsing Srinawk, Suchit and Paithun Wongthet, Witayakon Chiengkun, and Atsiri Dhammachote. The year in which she met Suchat Sawatsri, invented the writing persona "Sri Daoruang," and began her career as an author was 1973, the year in which university students and other champions of democracy "overthrew the . . . military government, [ushering] in the most exciting, chaotic, and ultimately painful period of Thai history in this century." (Phillips 1987: 8–9)

The very words "October 14" (*sipsi tula*/สิบสี่ตุลา), the day on which government troops fired upon and killed people demonstrating for greater political participation, provoke memories of terror and despair to this day. But these words also provoke memories of the unexpected, miraculous results of that day: the entire top leadership of the Thai government was forced to flee the country, and the next three years, before the brutal reestablishment of military power in October of 1976, were ". . . a period of intense, but chaotic, mobilization when all kinds of groups—new and old farmers' organizations, student groups, labor unions, political parties, public interest groups—vied with one another through demonstrations, strikes, rallies, and a variety of happenings to gain public support and . . . to begin . . . [the] process of [democratic] transformation." (Phillips 1987: 8)

Beyond the purely political aspects of the era, for Sri Daoruang, Suchat Sawatsri, and their colleagues, the 1970s comprised a decade of unprecedented opportunity for literary creativity. Life was extraordinary altogether, in those days, and, in its own way, rather simple, although awareness of this "simplicity" would occur to many of the participants only years later, in retrospect. I stress the emotional quality of this period of time because it is significant to certain plot elements and casual remarks that appear in the tales of the demon folk.

It is not too much to say that Sri Daoruang, of all the people writing about "the workers" at that time, was one of the very few who had actually worked in a factory, or as a servant. And she did these things as a matter of sheer survival, year after year—not temporarily, to save money for college, or as part of a social experiment, or as a show of solidarity with the masses. This is why the workers in many of her early stories "seem" so real; they were real, based on individuals she had known well and, in some cases, continued to know. Her fictional characters, like the human beings upon whom they were based, were less concerned with sweeping ideologies than with the mundane details of daily life. If there were social messages in Sri Daoruang's stories, they were implied, rather than being spelled out.

By contrast, many Thai authors whose work consciously pursued the goal of raising public consciousness about social problems tended to be didactic, conclusive, and prescriptive. Perhaps the most distinctive and important fact about this writer, when considered alongside her peers, is the fact about which she is most touchy: virtually all of them have at least a dozen years more of formal education than she has. Of course, there are other "working class" writers, in terms of origins; but all of them, including the women writers, began their literary careers in a college, on a scholarship, a circumstance that not only gave them an education, but propelled them into middle-class Thai life.

AMONG WOMEN WRITERS

How is Sri Daoruang to be "placed" among her female writing peers? In terms of occupation and achievement, the women who are described below are her peers; like her, they have won numerous awards for short stories and/or novels over the past twenty years. Additionally, each of them has won Thailand's most prestigious annual literary award: either the SEATO Award before 1979, or the SEA-Write Award which replaced it.

Suwanee Sukhontha (pen name of Suwanee Sukhon-thiang), to whom she wrote the touching memorial, "The

Letter You Never Received," was the daughter of a doctor in Phitsanuloke. She graduated from Silpakorn University in Bangkok, and taught art during the 1950s and early 1960s, before turning to literature. Her work was ground-breaking in its frank and often hilarious presentation of women's feelings about their relationships with friends, children, and lovers.

Kritsna Asokesin (pen name of Sukanya Cholsuk) gra-duated from Thammasat University after attending an exclusive girls' school. For the past thirty years, she has been writing witty, incisive novels of contemporary urban Thai life. The most popular of Kritsna's novels reveal the greedy underbelly of Thai middle-class society; her "anti-heroines" are would-be society matrons climbing the lad-der of social acceptance over the backs of neglected child-ren and disappointed husbands. In 1988, Kritsna was named a "National Artist," in the field of literature.

Anchan (pen name of Anchalee Vivathanachai) is the author of an excellent, controversial collection of short stories, *Anmani haeng chiwit* (Jewels of life/อัญมณีแห่งชีวิต) which won the SEAWrite Award in 1990. She graduated from Chulalongkorn University in the mid-1980s, and has done graduate work in English literature, in New York. Almost alone among Thai women writers, Anchan has bravely insisted on writing about such heretofore taboo subjects as the plight of battered women in Thai society, and women's sexual desires.

Botan (pen name of Supa Leusiri, now Supa Sirisingh) won the SEATO Award in 1967 for her first novel, *Chot-mai chak mueang Thai* (Letters from Thailand/จดหมาย-

จากเมืองไทย) at the age of twenty-one, and has been writing prolifically ever since.[5] Although she is a first-generation Chinese-Thai who grew up in Thonburi, a large city directly across the Chao Phraya River from Bangkok, in certain ways she has more in common with Sri Daoruang than do the writers named above, in terms of her modest origins; and they are close in age. However, despite the complete absence of emotional or financial support from her family, Botan was able to graduate from Chulalongkorn University by way of scholarships, and was working on her M.A. in Thai Literature at the time she wrote her award-winning novel. For many years, she and her husband have owned and operated the publishing company that produces her books. Her best-known novels focus on the lives of ambitious women who have risen above poverty and/or abuse to achieve autonomy in addition to worldly success.

I have presented these few biographical sketches to illustrate the literary company in which Sri Daoruang finds herself. I suggest that perhaps one ought not to be surprised if this writer demands, as she does, to be left alone to write her stories (she rarely appears in public), to work in her garden, and to dream of "a world in which one need never compete with anyone," nor try to live up to (or live down) a label such as "leftist" writer, or even "socially conscious" writer. Whether she is a "feminist" writer, however—by design, or by default—demands a

5. A revised edition of my translation of this novel was published by Silkworm Books, Chiang Mai, in 2002.

fuller discussion, which I shall undertake following the tales of the demon folk.

CHAPTER TWO

From *Ramayana* to *Ramakian* to Tales of the Demon Folk

FROM *RAMAYANA* TO *RAMAKIAN*

The *Ramakian* is one of many versions of the *Ramayana*, the great epic that was composed by "Valmiki" in India, about two thousand years ago.[1] This epic may have been carried to Thailand by way of Bengal and Burma; or it may have come by way of the kingdoms and principalities that have come to comprise Indonesia and Malaysia today. To be sure, there are versions of the *Ramayana* in all of these countries. What is certain, in the case of Siam (as

1. English translations and versions of the *Ramakian* (also spelled *Ramakien*) upon which I have drawn include Cadet 1975, Puri 1949, Raghavan 1980, the Chalermnit edition of the Rama I version (identified in the bibliography under "Rama I"), and Shastri 1990. Thai versions include Premseri 1977, and the Thai text included in Bofman 1984 and in Shastri 1990. I have also referred to essays on characters in the *Ramakian* by Chinda 1990, Chusak, 1993, and Srisurang and Sumalaya 1982.

Thailand was known until 1938) is that tales of Prince Ram were familiar as early as the thirteenth century. The third king of the Sukhothai period, during whose reign the written Thai language was developed, was named Ramkhamhaeng (?1279–1298).

During the succeeding era of Siamese history, the Ayutthaya period (from the fourteenth century to 1782 C.E.), dramatizations of the *Ramayana/Ramakian* tales were performed at court, and undoubtedly existed in written form. Not surprisingly, to many Siamese the very name of the capital city of Ayutthaya has seemed a reasonable testimony to the Siamese origins of the tale, for everyone knows that it was in Ayutthaya (in India, Ayodhya) that the great Prince Ram was born; and that he married Princess Sida, the most beautiful and virtuous woman in the world, and met many adventures as the result of her abduction by the wicked king of the demons, Thotsakan.[2]

Virtually all Siamese written records were destroyed when Ayutthaya was sacked by the Burmese in 1767. One of the great accomplishments of the succeeding early Thonburi period (1767–1782) and the current, Bangkok (or "Rattanakosin") period (1782–present) was the reconstruction of Thai written literature, based upon the amazing memories of surviving members of the Ayutthaya court. General Chakri, crowned King of Siam in 1782,

---

2. In Thai, ทศกัณฐ์. This character is called "Ravana" in the Indian versions of the *Ramayana*. In the *Ramakian* the chief characters are known by more than one name. For examples, "Tosapak" also refers to Thotsakan. They also are referred to by a variety of descriptive terms.

had more than literary objectives in mind when he and his courtiers began the great task of composing the first complete version of the *Ramakian*. According to historian David Wyatt:

> [The] chief monument of [literature of the First Reign of the Bangkok period] . . . is usually taken to be the enormous *Ramakian* . . . which Rama I and his courtiers set to verse in 1797 . . . This is no blind translation of an Indian text, but rather a recasting of a classic central to Indian civilization in such a way that it was domesticated into Siamese tradition. The central figure in the *Ramayana* is, after all, a Rama (not completely alien to Rama I) who lives in a city called Ayodhya (or Ayudhya) and ascends his throne through virtue and bravery after a long dark period of dangerous warfare. The point is, however, that the characters and setting of the *Ramakian*, no less than the language, is clearly Siamese. (Wyatt 1984: 153–54)

Not only the performing arts but the visual arts were involved in the institutionalization of the *Ramakian* as a primary component of Siamese literary history, and as a validation of the legitimacy of the new Chakri dynasty.

> Rama I commissioned the painting of a set of murals that depicted episodes from the *Ramakian* [encircling the interior gallery of the Temple of the Emerald Buddha]. When celebrations associated with the image of the Emerald Buddha were held, he saw to it that performances

of episodes from the *Ramakian* story were included. In visual and ritual terms a clear message was being sent. The "Glory of Rama" had now been incorporated into the Buddhist ideal of royal power and authority manifested in the Emerald Buddha on the one hand and in the reigning dynasty on the other. (Reynolds 1991: 58)

The original, Indian version of the *Ramayana* naturally had reflected the Hindu orientation of the poet who wrote it, and his society. In Thailand, Reynolds writes:

When the literary, performative, iconic, and cultic aspects of the *Ramakian* tradition are all taken fully into account, it is necessary to conclude that this rendition of the Rama story—at least since its reformulation in the late eighteenth century—tilts more toward Buddhism than Hinduism." (Reynolds 1991: 59)

Over the centuries, the *Ramakian* has been told through the magnificent court drama of the *khon* (โขน), in which the actors wear gorgeous costumes and masks. Ordinary villagers, however, know the *Ramakian* through the shadow puppet theater, or *nang*; through temple art such as the murals at the Temple of the Emerald Buddha; and through the performances of *"likay"* or *"like."*[3] The *like* is a kind of itinerant burlesque; to this day, traveling theater

---

3. I have chosen to use the English spellings *khon* (masked theater), *nang* (shadow puppet theater), and *like* (folk theater), for the Thai terms โขน, หนัง, ลิเก, respectively.

troupes perform *like* on the grounds of temples all over Thailand, and make the classics—or, to be more precise, low-budget and high-humor versions of the classics—familiar to people from all walks and stations of life.

It was through the *like* that Sri Daoruang first became familiar with the chief characters and some of the tales of the *Ramakian*. She remembers these performances:

People in the country who don't have theaters don't see performances very often. The *khon, nang* [shadow play], *like,* and movies are all parts of the [festivities surrounding] Buddhist ordinations, weddings, funerals, and temple fairs. Everyone—that is, everyone who is as old as I am now—recognizes the *Ramakian*, because of such events. *Khon* is the most expensive of all these forms of theater. Nowadays, one may see it only at the National Theater in Bangkok.

Like features the *Ramakian* and other stories as well, unlike *khon*, which features only the *Ramakian*, and only certain episodes of that, of course, because it is so long. The gestures of the *khon* performers as they dance, their costumes, the dances themselves, the fighting, all are very beautiful. In the old days, children would watch the *khon*, and then go home and play at imitating the actions of the performers. I liked Hanuman better than Ram, because he was quick, strong, and smart. What do you think? Without Hanuman, do you think Ram could have beaten the demons?

Like nowadays continues to perform episodes from the *Ramakian*, but it is difficult to find. The troupes prefer to perform other works, because they are not as demanding as the *Ramakian*. Children the age of my son Mon don't recognize even Hanuman—because their mothers never take them to see *khon*! What characters do children recognize today? Only [the Japanese television cartoon characters] Dora-emon and Sei-ya . . . (Wan Pen 1993: 261)

Following is a brief synopsis of the *Ramakian*—or rather, of those parts of it that must be understood in order to appreciate what Sri Daoruang has done with the original story, and the original characters, in constructing her contemporary "Tales of the demon folk." The significance of specific plot elements and characterizations will be explored in chapter 4, following the short stories. If the information that follows seems to have something of a "once upon a time" quality, that is intended, reflecting Sri Daoruang's own interpretation of the story that she learned —not from books. but from the magical, theatrical experience of the *like*.

THE *RAMAKIAN*

Unfairly deprived of his throne by the machinations of his stepmother, banished from the great city of Ayutthaya, Prince Ram set off into the world, accompanied by his loyal brother, Prince Lak, and his faithful wife Sida. At their wedding, he had described her thus:

Her face was as bright as a star, her eyebrows were bent

in a perfect curve as drawn by an artist. Her eyes were
[as] beautiful as those of a bashful doe. Her nose was
perfectly and beautifully fresh. Her ears were perfect.
Her mouth was like a budding flower. Her hair, her
cheeks, her breasts, her manner . . . were all perfect and
finely shaped and there was not a single spot in the whole
of her body where any criticism could be made . . .
(Rama I 1967: 32–33)

Eventually, the three came to live in a humble hermitage
on the banks of the river Godavari. One day, a demoness
named Samanakha, sister of the demon king Thotsakan,
came upon their camp. This demoness, notorious for her
insatiable sexual appetites, had recently become widowed
(when Thotsakan himself accidentally slew her husband);
now, she was searching the world for a new lover. In the
disguise of a beautiful woman, she came to the place
where Ram, Lak, and Sida made their abode.

At the very first sight she fell in desperate love with the
prince of Ayudhya. But Rama was irresponsive to her
amorous display. When [Samanakha] got a glimpse of
Sida, she at once understood . . . (Puri and Charoen
1949: 33)

But Samanakha was to suffer more than wounded pride.
Not only was Prince Ram "irresponsive" to her "amorous
display"; he responded with frank disgust, whereupon
Samanakha flew into a rage, reverted to her hideous demonic form, and attacked Sida. Instantly, Ram and Lak

went to Sida's defense, cutting off Samanakha's ears, nose, hands, and feet. It was this incident which incited the desire of the demon princess for revenge, which in turn led to the disaster of Sida's abduction, and the wars that followed.

Returning to Thotsakan's court, Samanakha described her abduction and rape by Ram and Lak. This blow at his own honor irritated Thotsakan, but his anger was soon eclipsed by curiosity, for he never could resist the opportunity to seduce a beautiful woman, and his sister described Sida, Prince Ram's wife, as beautiful beyond description, lovelier than any woman in the world, even more desirable than Thotsakan's own beloved consort Montho, or any of the eighty-four thousand other women in his palace, all of whom adored him and rejoiced in his inexhaustible sexual prowess. Although Thotsakan, like all demons, had many heads—ten, in his case, each one more frightening and horrible than the next, and also twenty arms—when he chose to assume human form, he was remarkably handsome. Unfortunately, when he became enraged he would return to his true demonic form, just as his sister Samanakha had done when she "forgot herself" and attacked Sida.

> I was bringing [Sida] as a gift to you . . . when [that] arrogant Laksmana pounced upon me and having disfigured me snatched her away from me. Therefore, you go quickly and bring this lady of charming loveliness, and having taken revenge for my disgrace rejoice yourself with this wife of Rama. (Shastri 1990: 251)

Thotsakan, obsessed with his fantasies of Sida, managed at last to capture her by means of magic, and spirit her away to his palace in Lanka. Ram, discovering that Sida had been stolen away, pledged to recapture his wife and avenge his honor by destroying the king of the demons. His most important allies in this quest were his brother Lak, and also the magically endowed monkey Hanuman, who led his formidable monkey troops into the fray.

Hanuman, son of a monkey mother and fathered by the god of the wind, is a remarkable character in the *Ramakian*, and has always been the favorite of *like* aficionados. He is clever, amusing, and full of tricks; but he is also fierce in battle, perfectly loyal, and indestructible.

Sida, imprisoned in Thotsakan's pleasure garden, will have nothing to do with the lovesick demon. He offers all that he has—not only his passion and devotion, but worldly goods beyond imagining:

> You are the center of my life / I feel great affection for you, beautiful lady. / It almost kills me . . . I am inviting you, lovely one, / To enter the sandalwood palace / Decorated with endless precious things, Like a heavenly city, / Together with the ladies-in-waiting, / Eighty-four thousand young women, / I will keep you as chief queen, / Sharing the sparkling white umbrella. / You will be superior to all the maidens. / Young one, have pity on me. (Bofman 1984: 121–22)

But Sida's response gives him no hope of pity.

Why do you come and insult / The Arrow-bearer, the
Summit of the World / The Lord of the Naga Throne? /
The Avatar will come and destroy the giants / To put an
end to the race of evil . . . / Your body is an evil one / Its
ten heads and ten faces will be cut off / The day you stole
me and brought me here / You survived only because
you fled / If you were slow you would have been killed
. . . (Bofman 1984: 123)

The more she reviles and insults him, the more obsessed
he becomes. Frank E. Reynolds has written,

In some tellings of the tale Ravana is presented as a
thoroughly evil character with no redeeming virtues. In
others he is more a kind of flawed hero whose demise,
though necessary and appropriate, is not devoid of truly
tragic dimensions. (Reynolds 1991: 52)

In the Thai version, this is certainly the case. Indeed, in
some respects Thotsakan is the most "human" of all the
characters in the *Ramakian*.

One day, alone and despairing in the beautiful garden
that was her prison, Sida attempts to hang herself. Just in
time, Hanuman, who has been searching for her throughout the demon kingdom of Lanka, finds her and saves her
life. He offers to take her to Ram at once, but she refuses.

Look, brave Hanuman, / Your words aren't right. / Why
do you think things are so easy? / You didn't think with

wisdom. / Totsapak [Thotsakan] kidnapped me and fled. / This fact is a source of suspicion. / In addition, you came / To take me from the city of the devil. / It would add to my guilt. / My guilt would spread in all direc-tions. / Even the Avatar King [Ram] / Would hear and be suspicious . . . tell His Majesty to hurry here / And kill Totsapak / And end his royal race. / Then I will leave Lanka / And attend court at the feet of [Ram]. (Bofman 1984: 140)

It is interesting that Sida, renowned for her beauty, virtue, and demure behavior, is nevertheless permitted to show anger, resentment, and suspicion, and exhibit a variety of behaviors that ordinarily would be considered unbecoming in a woman, much less a princess. Yet, such emotions and behaviors are approved—so long as they are in Prince Ram's interest. The effort to remain the most virtuous of wives justifies behavior and words that verge on stridency.

After many adventures and battles, Ram and his allies kill Thotsakan, Sida rejoins Prince Ram in Ayutthaya, and he claims his throne. Unfortunately, the virtuous prince cannot rid himself of the suspicion that Sida has been unfaithful to him during her captivity in Lanka, and he is certain that his subjects also are suspicious. Sida, humiliated and outraged when she learns of his feelings, demands to go through the fire ceremony: only a pure woman would be able to walk unharmed through the fire. She emerges from the fire lovelier than ever, and Ram is satisfied—for a time, until the crafty Samanakha surfaces once again, disguised as Sida's maid, and asks her to draw a picture of Thotsakan from memory.

No sooner had [Sida] finished the drawing than the revengeful she-demon disappeared from her sight and entered into the figure on the slate. At that very moment Ram returned from his sojourn. In consternation, Sida tried to wipe the figure out, but to her utter dismay the more she wiped, the more vivid did the figure appear. Puzzled, she hid the slate under the bed. (Puri and Charoen 1949: 111)

Finding the incriminating slate, Ram is convinced that indeed he has been cuckolded by the ten-headed demon. He orders Lak to take Sida deep into the forest and kill her; but Lak, unable to bring himself to do the unjust deed, brings back the heart of a deer. "Rama saw the heart and the only comment that came out of his extremely jealous lips was that her heart was as ugly as a beast's." (Puri and Charoen 1949: 114)

Eventually, Ram and Sida are again reconciled; yet, Sida remains bitter. "Rama asked her forgiveness and entreated her to return to the palace, but Sida was tired of Rama's so-called kindness." (Puri and Charoen 1949: 119) Sida even succeeds in magically disappearing through the floor and reappearing in the land of Patal, in answer to a prayer she has uttered. (Puri and Charoen 1949: 122) Yet, at the end of the tale, the gods intervene to effect a final reconciliation between the two. (This seemingly "tacked on" reconciliation does not occur in all of the many versions of the *Ramayana* that are told in South and Southeast Asia.)

The reader (or the audience, in the case of *khon* or *like*), is offered no glimpse of Sida's thoughts at the end of the tale, as she complies with the gods' dictum and makes her final decision to forgive, once and for all, the continuing suspicion of her self-righteous husband. She sees clearly what he has done, and what she has unfairly suffered. But then, she gives in.

> [Rama] readily confessed his guilt and asked for Sida's pardon. Sida was still far from showing any mercy. She was too cut to the quick to forgive or forget . . . His good and bad were so changing that she could not believe herself in Rama's hand which might at any moment be raised to fall heavily upon her.
>
> Nevertheless . . . she at last gave way and showed her readiness to accept Rama in her favour. No sooner had the words come out of Sida's lips than Rama's heart was overwhelmed with joy. (Puri and Charoen 1949: 125)

Whatever Sida may have felt in her heart was left to the imagination. But Sri Daoruang, in writing her tales of the demon folk, decided to tell everything from Sida's point of view.

FROM *RAMAKIAN* TO TALES OF THE DEMON FOLK

How do Sri Daoruang's contemporary tales differ, at the most apparent level, from the *Ramakian*? To begin with, Sida is not the wife of the supremely virtuous and moralistic Ram. Instead, she has chosen as her mate the irascible, lusty, eminently fallible and occasionally pathetic Thotsakan. Like her namesake, Sri Daoruang's modern Sida is loving and faithful, but given to moods of doubt and frustration; she occasionally becomes bitter over her dependence upon her "lord," and she has a sharp tongue. We are given frequent glimpses into her private thoughts, which, often enough, are not reflected in her behavior to the other characters, least of all to her "beloved demon."

Despite all, Sri Daoruang's Thotsakan and Sida are clearly recognizable as folk from the *Ramakian*, even if they are surrounded by the sometimes dismaying vistas of contemporary urban Thailand rather than by the fabled vistas of Lanka. The background music of these tales is not the stately, hypnotic accompaniment of the classical *khon* orchestra, but a cacophonous symphony comprised of the unceasing blare of the tape recorders of Sida and Thotsakan's neighbors; the banal, ear-splitting daily messages that blare from loudspeakers at the nearby district office; and the grating voices of the Japanese TV cartoon superheroes their son Hanuman adores.

In the original *Ramakian*, Hanuman was the faithful ally of Prince Ram and had nothing to do with Thotsakan—except to help plot and carry out his defeat. But in Sri Daoruang's tales, Thotsakan and Sida have a son, and his name is Hanuman. As I have stated in chapter 1, Sri Daoruang's only son was born with multiple heart defects; unending anxiety over his precarious health has been a major factor in her life. The Hanuman of the *Ramakian* is not only amusing and endearing, but indestructible. The Hanuman of Sri Daoruang's tales is amusing and endearing, but frail. The story, "Thotsakan Puts Down the *Chingchoks*" reflects upon the significance of their son "Hanuman's" birth, and the profound effect of his precarious health during infancy and early childhood upon his parents. How wonderful it would have been for them both if this child, despite the profound physical challenges with which he was born, had been, despite all, indestructible.

Despite the many circumstances and events that are obviously drawn from the author's life, it would be a mistake to read Sri Daoruang's "Tales of the Demon Folk" as autobiographical, for these are tales filled with invention and fantasy. "One reason writing is hard," Sri Daoruang has written, "is that one is mired in lavish private dreams, dreaming within oneself these stories and words, words, words . . . dreaming all the time, and there is no end of it until there is an end of us." (Kepner 1995)

Where the "real events" of this author's life begin and end, and where her "lavish private dreams" intrude, to refashion and refine those events, can never be known.

CHAPTER THREE

Tales of the Demon Folk
Thotsakan and Sida

When Thotsakan and Sida exchanged words of anger for the first time, their son Hanuman was stricken with confusion and sorrow. He sat midway between his father and mother, holding an old picture album he had picked up from the shelf beside the chest, turning it over in his hands before opening it. In the album, Sida had arranged photographs in careful order, from long ago to the present. Hanuman opened the album to the first page and let his gaze move slowly over the pictures, but his heart was not in it.

Thotsakan, leaning against the wall with his arms crossed, could not help glancing at the open page, could not look away from the image of himself as a young fellow. And in that moment, he was seized with regret— for his lost youth, and for the past. Thotsakan felt that those years ought to stand as some sort of—well, some sort of assurance, in his wife's eyes. He also felt that she ought to accept his status as the head of this family more than she did. There he was, on the album page, a strapping lad, dark complected, with strong features. Beneath heavy brows, his large eyes looked half-lidded, as if he were winking—that is, winking on one side of his face. If one looked carefully, one could see that Thotsakan's gaze projected one sort of nature from the left eye, and another sort of nature from the right eye; he looked to be all temper and ferocity on the one side—and softness, kindness, and understanding on the other.

At the time this picture was taken, Thotsakan was a young man who had cherished his single state for thirty years. He had been an eager if unparticular lover about whom it was said, "*Ai* Thot, eh?[1] If he feels around and doesn't find a tail, she'll do." But he had competed with many young men to win, at last, the heart of the young woman named Sida, a fatherless orphan, a seamstress in the largest dressmaking establishment in the market and younger than himself by one cycle. Once he had established a household with Sida, Thotsakan had forsaken his bachelor ways absolutely; but then, as the legend tells us, Sida was utterly lovely, so lovely that *Ai Khaek* "Ramalak" had spent a fortune and even gone to battle, not once but many times, because of her.[2]

These days, however, Thotsakan and Sida shared their lives without obstacles of any kind to hinder them. In fact,

1. *Ai* is a familiar prefix for a man's name. It is commonly used in rural areas, but in Bangkok it has a pejorative connotation.
2. *Khaek* is a slang term for "Indian"; literally, the word means "guest."

the two of them had become a veritable model of husband and wife, a couple to whom their neighbors invariably referred when they spoke of honesty, endurance, hard work, thrift, and high principles. Both of them came of poor families. No jewels had they, nor a single revealing birthmark.[3] Their loving hearts were the only dowry they brought to their marriage.

Yes, once he had taken upon himself the duties and obligations of father and husband, head of the family, Thotsakan had forsaken the pursuit of selfish pleasures, whether that meant playing *mak-ruk* (chess), or *takhro lot buang* (takraw), or riding his bicycle past the movie theater to flirt with the attractive young females who stood out front. The drinking of liquor, the tossing of tasty bits of grilled fish into his mouth, all such pleasures he gladly eschewed upon the birth of his son. He was content to live quietly with his wife and his boy, and work ever harder to keep up with the soaring cost of living. Both husband and wife were determined not to owe anything to anyone, or to give in to the desire for luxuries and buy on credit. Thotsakan's monthly salary of four thousand baht provided no modern conveniences or dinners in fancy restaurants, but they did not feel at all poor—for did they not have hot rice to eat and a soft bed to sleep on? Every day when Thotsakan came home from work, Sida met

3. Sri Daoruang is making fun of Thai romance novels in which it is discovered that the poor, embattled heroine is actually the daughter of a rich and powerful family. An old family retainer recognizes her by a birthmark.

him at the door with a glass of cool water. Life, in his opinion, was excellent, and he felt contentment and a sense of quiet pride when he thought of himself as the "shade of the po tree, shade of the banyan tree," under which his little family was able to live a contented and happy life.

Time passed . . . Life was happy some of the time, sad some of the time, as it is for all human creatures. When Hanuman, their only child, completed *mathayom* 3 (grade 9), Sida expressed the opinion that he ought to leave school for awhile, and work; and it was this opinion that led to harsh words between his father, who insisted that Hanuman continue his education immediately, and his mother, who pointed out that he could return to school easily enough, after a season of work. Moreover, Sida was thinking of going to work herself!

Truly, Thotsakan loved Sida and their son very much, even if Thotsakan was sometimes grumpy when he came home from work, exhausted at the end of the day. Why, he wondered, was she doing this? Why had she begun this campaign of rebellion, this stubborness? When she had first brought up the matter, uncomfortable suspicions had begun to invade his mind.

"Are you feeling ill?" Sida had asked.

"No. There's nothing wrong with me," he had replied hastily. "Why do you ask?"

"I noticed that you look pale, that's all. *Khun* . . . er . . . I thought—well, what I want to say is that I have been thinking of looking for work myself."

At those words, Thotsakan's heart had dropped. What

was this? His own Sida, telling him his health was not good, his body not strong! She thought that he looked pale, and sick, and weak—such a poor fellow that she must go and work outside their home. Eh . . . Sida had never been like this before, no, never.

"Why do you want to go out and work? Don't you have enough to eat, from one day to the next?" His temper was rising fast.

Sida gently laid her arm across his shoulder. "It is only that I have watched you coming home so tired, for so long. When our son was small, I thought only about caring for him. Now he is grown, and I have free time— why shouldn't I help out? Rice grows more expensive by the day, and everything else too. Our son will have opportunities to study further, just as you wish . . . But for now, if you are the only one working, before you know it you will make yourself ill from working too much, and then the whole family will suffer."

The conversation on that day made Thotsakan feel quite distant from Sida. That her words were reasonable did not make him want to listen to them. He did not want to hear that he could not provide for his family. No doubt the monthly budget, which had never interested him, was now going to be dragged before his eyes, whether he would look at it or not.

"And where do you think you would find a job?" he continued. "What do you know? Let me assure you that the ones doing the hiring don't want people your age. They only want to hire young women."

"I thought . . . sewing," Sida said softly.

35

"Aw-w . . . You want to go out of your home and sew in some shop, is that it?" His fury was increasing by the moment. "Where they can all say, 'Well, now we see that Thotsakan can't support his family!' And where will you get the money to dress yourself to go to this shop? Or to pay the bus fare? Where will you find the money for something to eat with your rice, at lunch time? And another thing—if you go out of our home early in the morning, and the both of us return at night quite exhausted, then what? When I return home in a foul mood, and you are in a foul mood as well from your sewing job, I ask you—in such a situation, where is the comfort and happiness of the home to come from? Answer me that!"

Sida continued to sit quietly, gazing out the window and thinking, "He thinks that I will give in to him, as usual . . ."

"The fact is that we simply do not have enough money," she said, in that maddeningly reasonable, cool tone of voice she liked to use during arguments. "You know very well how much everything costs nowadays."

"Then why don't you economize?" Thotsakan asked, as if this were a solution. "Other men bring home less money every month, and their families seem to survive. Perhaps it isn't necessary to go upcountry quite so often . . ."

At this reference to the few trips she made to visit her very own mother, Sida lowered her head, and felt the tears well up hotly in her eyes. Oh, how she hated having to depend upon him! Her thoughts drifted to the past, and she was struck with wonder: in those days, when they were first together, everything had been so—different from the way it was now, everything had seemed so easy then, so clear . . .

Ten years before, there had been only the two of them. Thotsakan's salary was a little over two thousand baht. Over the years, it had gone up steadily, until today it was double that amount. But the cost of living had much more than doubled, while Thotsakan's strength had steadily, naturally declined. Oh, the stubbornness of the man! He would not think of accepting his wife's sympathy—oh, no! He would continue to go into battle with the "Ramalaks" of the marketplace, again and again, all by himself.

The wind was changing direction . . . Thotsakan considered how to escape from the problem that faced him. But his view of the situation was entirely different from Sida's. Each considered what to do next, but it did not occur to either of them that they might sit down together, and find a compromise. Sida thought only of working as a seamstress, and bringing more money into the family; Thotsakan thought only of how he might recapture the former warmth and happiness of his home, and make things exactly as they had been before. Thotsakan thought hard—and then, he made a momentous decision.

Here it is, look! A color television set—see? A fourteen-inch screen! And there—look! A gas stove with four burners, and an oven besides. These were the machines that supplied convenience, and also modern happiness, and they were the first of their kind to enter the household of Thotsakan and Sida. A catalog displaying the newest refrigerators from Japan lay enticingly on one piece of the new suite of living room furniture. You choose, Sida! Which refrigerator do you want? Whatever you want, they have it!

The sulky look on Thotsakan's face had been replaced by a merry grin. Up-to-date clothes in the latest styles and more or less splendid household accessories began to proliferate in the home of Thotsakan and Sida. In other words, they had become like their neighbors. Despite his modest salary, Thotsakan had been able to buy a houseful of conveniences and luxuries in return for a lifetime of debt. Thus did the modern family increase the happiness and quality of life, along with the monthly payments. But Sida did not grin merrily; no, she looked sad, and was very quiet.

"Kan, how much longer will you have to make payments on these things from *Ai Khaek* Ramalak? Now he wants to bring in a wi-dee-oh, and let us use it to see how we like it. I don't want a wi-dee-oh! I want only the things we need."

Thotsakan's face clouded with an expression somewhere between confusion, melancholy, and anger. He expelled a great sigh, and lowered himself to the floor heavily.

"Oh dear, I can't do anything right," Sida said, her voice full of both sorrow and exasperation. "I don't know what you want, Kan. You don't like this, you don't want that—and look at all of these things! I can't keep up with you—"

"No, you can't—and do you want to know why? Because I'm old, that's why!" And then he roared at her: "Ta-a-a-a-w-w-w!" and the wrathful side of his face overwhelmed the cool, sweet side so that it seemed that everything upon which his gaze fell must surely burst into flame. "Ta-a-a-a-w-w-w ! But I am not so old that I can't handle a few other women—how would you like that, eh?" She feared that his rage would burn out of control altogether, but she too was angry.

"Go ahead, then—go find your 'few other women'!" she snapped. But as soon as the harsh words had left her lips, she regretted them, and said, "Oh, Kan—how can I talk to you? As for the matter of my going to work—I don't have to work outside our home, you know. We live in a row house, and we're near the main road. Maybe we're not so close to the market, but we live on a busy lane. All I need to do is put up a sign that I take in sewing,—and I could sell sweets, too. Hanuman could help me. It would bring in enough money to make a difference with the household expenses. We are both growing older every day, Kan, not only you, and we don't even own this house. I am not going to argue with you about this anymore. I'm going to do what I need to do."

Sida wanted to add, "I love you," but the words would not come.

—

.Thotsakan lay awake nearly all night after his beloved wife had told him that she did not want to go to work only to be away from their home. No, it was only the money she cared about! What was he, in his wife's eyes? He felt that his status, his role as head of the household was shrinking away to nothing. He lay with one arm over his forehead, deep in thought.

—

"Hanuman . . . bring that fabric and stack it over here.

Then you can go out with this sweet—I have it all wrapped and ready. Oh, we forgot to buy that thread I wanted this morning. Now I shall have to finish the dress tonight. You know whose dress I'm talking about—while you're out, be sure to stop by and tell her it will be ready by tomorrow evening."

Nearly six months passed, during which Sida was strong and resourceful. She sewed, she made sweets to sell. She and Hanuman worked hard together. In the little time she had, she tried to please her demon in every way she could, but there were times when Sida had to allow Thotsakan to return to something of the life he had known in his youth . . . As for Thotsakan, he was not a little annoyed to find the home which once had been quite tidy littered with scraps of cloth from the sewing of dresses, and scraps of paper and banana leaf from the making of sweets. And yet, he felt himself to be at something of a loss for words when, returning from work or from a few beers he had consumed along the way, his wife and son were clearly happy to see him, and took pains to make him comfortable. True, when the two of them were busily rushing about, he scarcely knew where to put himself, or whether it would be a good idea to offer his help, or not. (Certainly, he could not use a sewing machine!) But Sida seemed to understand, and would make some thoughtful comment such as, "Kan, why don't you go watch the Muppets on TV, and I'll be finished with this sewing in a few minutes." Or, "Are you hungry,

Kan? There's some nice tapioca with pork tripe in the cupboard. Hanuman, go fix a nice bowl for your papa . . ."

Thotsakan had had no experience with such a level of activity and confusion. He knew that his wife and son were tired from their labors, and that sewing all day and night was not something anyone did for fun. But he did not know what to do about any of these goings-on. What he found most irksome were the times when his own wife's name sometimes came up, when he was at the bar with the other demons.

"*Ai* Yak[4]—your wife is not only beautiful but hard-working, and I am jealous as hell! Why do you think I sit here drinking? Because my wife stands around doing nothing all day, with her bare hands open and waiting to be filled, that's why."

"But it's a nuisance, I tell you," Thotsakan replied irritably. "I used to have a quiet home, and now it's nothing but work, work all day. It isn't good enough for her, keeping a nice home—no, she has to show off how tired she is, from working all day."

"Eh? Listen, my friend, I tell you that she's right," his demon companion offered. "If my own wife had the same idea, would I complain? Not with two of us spending—and two of us earning!

Not long after, on another evening in the tavern, someone remarked that *Ai Yak* Thotsakan hadn't been around, lately.

⚊

4. *Yak* means demon or giant.

"What color thread do you need?" Thotsakan asked. "Why can't I go and pick it up?"

Mother and son sat staring at each other.

"And I don't know why you can't show me how to wrap those sweets," he added, with a sheepish grin.

"Oh, you don't have to do that. You're already tired from working all day. Really, we can do these things ourselves. It isn't hard, working the way Hanuman and I do here at home. We work some, then we rest some. It's easy." Sida looked down as she spoke so that Thotsakan could not see the expression in her eyes, and therefore he was not sure how to answer her.

"See, Mama?" Hanuman asked brightly. "Our hero has come to help us! Now, I'll be able to go to the Adult School."

"So, you think you have saved enough already?" Sida asked him.

"Yes! You give me money every day," he said proudly.

His mother beamed, but his father's face fell. "What about the money I give you, son?"

Sida replied for Hanuman. "He uses the money you give him, and he saves the money he earns working with me— all of it. He's a smart boy, your son is," she added, glancing proudly at Hanuman from the corner of her eye.

The boy grinned at his papa. "Don't you think it's the right thing to do, Papa? After all, one has to have a present before one can have a future!"

This was a favorite slogan from a television commercial much admired by Hanuman, only son of Mr. Thotsakan and his wife Sida.

—

And now, you have seen a beginning, taken from somewhere in the middle of a legend, the legend of Thotsakan and Sida, and some other folks, a legend which appears to be unfinished. Who, one wonders, will be waiting to see the next act?

(*Lok nangsue* [Book world] 2527/1984)

Thotsakan Puts Down the *Chingchoks*

Every one of us has some activity, or some thing, that is most important to us, even precious. It may be the work we do for a living, or work we do just for the pleasure of it. Some people find their joy in raising healthy roosters, feeding them up and training them until they are robust enough to go out and kill other roosters in combat. Some people like to re-arrange their furniture, while others find relaxation and pleasure in assembling a circle of their friends at home, opening a few bottles, playing tapes of their favorite music loudly, and shouting at each other in what they define as conversation. There are those who think it a great pleasure to go out about the town in search of delectable edibles—and indeed, there a great many delectable edibles to be found, about town.

At the time of which I write, and continuing to this very day, Hanuman, the son of Thotsakan and Sida, when he is free from his chores, loves to sit and draw pictures. His favorite subjects are tanks and robot people. Or, he might take his plastic soccer ball outdoors and kick it around with his friends. As for his mother Sida, what she enjoys is puzzling over the dress patterns in the weekly magazines; or working in her garden, planting peppers and eggplant, ginger and galanga and lemon grass . . . She adheres strictly to the policies of thrift encouraged by the Municipal Government of Lanka, as exemplified by the stirring songs incorporated in the radio "news" which urge all good citizens to plant kitchen gardens, so that they need never fear going hungry. When she is weary from digging in the dirt, Sida hums the catchy refrain to herself three times: "No need to go to market . . . no need to go to market . . . no need to go to market . . ." and then—*o-o-o-om . . . piang*!!—her weariness simply vanishes!

As for Thotsakan, her dear demon, the like of whom is not to be seen, there is one activity he has enjoyed ever since he was a small boy. He loves to read and to collect books. He once confessed to Uncle Fai, the hermit who lives next door, that when he was a boy he even stole money from his own mother to buy comics—until she caught him. But did the stripes of the switch stop him? Not at all. He stole books out of stores! Even when he didn't have time to read them, he could admire them and, what was most important, they were his.

Not only does Thotsakan collect books, he cares for them meticulously, making special dust jackets for them. Even as a boy, he filled many shelves with books: comics, movie magazines, books about politics, funeral books, novels and collections of tales, and a good number of magazines that explore "the science of gender," which he bought for the pictures. He even saved those printed advertisements that vendors force upon people, in the streets. And all of these, he treasured to the extent that his wife and child were not allowed to touch them, for he feared that their hands, which were ignorant of the value of his treasures, would do them injury.

Thotsakan even built a special small room, his library—his private world—greatly impressing his friends (whose remarks nonetheless tended, as usual, to the sardonic and faintly disparaging) and also impressing Nai Ong-In, the carpenter who built the room and all of the shelves within it, and fitted the screens. Thotsakan might sleep under a mosquito net in his own bedroom, but his library must be fitted with screens.

"That's where your major wife sleeps," Sida teased him, "the beloved wife no one dare touch!" To which Thotsakan the Dreamer replied, "If you would rather see a flesh and blood version, let me know."

Every day after his library had been completed, Thotsakan would return home, and before he took the time to wash his face, much less sit down and rest, he would change his clothes and disappear into his room full of books. He would lovingly wipe the dust from their jackets with his fingers, or wipe them against the clean cotton of the *phakhaoma* that covered his backside; and if he noticed so much as a mosquito dropping, he would lift the hem of the *phakhaoma* and, with a tiny bit of spit, efface the offending spot.[1] Yet, despite the attention he gave to these

1. A *phakhaoma* is a long wide strip of plaid cloth worn by men as a wrap around and used for a variety of purposes.

precious possessions, he felt himself to be at the mercy of a band of monstrous enemies over which, try as he might, he could not achieve victory. Not only were the screens unable to keep out every speck of dust; they were unable to keep out mosquitoes, cockroaches, mice, and *chingchoks* (house lizards).

Thotsakan had told the carpenter in no uncertain terms that he wanted not so much as a crack or cranny in his library, through which such creatures would be able to gain entrance. And Nai Ong-In had given his word. "I guarantee it, sir! Not an ant will be able to get into that room." He had then turned to his boy helper and added, in a whisper, "Anyway, if the ants do get in there, the *chingchoks* will eat them."

Thotsakan was well acquainted with the deadpan humor of Nai Ong-In, who had once solemnly announced that the famous comedian Lotok had been in his house, even though he had pointedly told his son that he did not want this man in his house because he didn't like Lotok's face. And, because any time Lotok was around, nobody from his house or from the house next door got any work done because all they wanted to do was sit around, in his house, and watch Lotok, until he had got plain sick and fed up with it. But the boy wouldn't listen, and so there had been nothing to do but pick up the damned television set and haul it to the pawn shop. Since that day, Lotok's face had not been seen in Nai Ong-In's house.

Thotsakan decided that he would believe the man's promises. But, perhaps because Thotsakan and Sida had never before lived in a house in which one room was fitted with screens, they were unprepared for certain things. Such as the way in which the excited and curious mosquitoes would all but form a queue in hopes of gaining entrance, clustering in great dark, feverish clouds before the screens. And there, naturally, the *chingchoks* would congregate to hunt their prey, though they scarcely needed hunting. Although Thotsakan would try to open the screen door ever so slowly and carefully, whenever he did so the entire gang of predatory *chingchoks* would become terrified and flee in terror—running for their lives straight into the library. As for the neat plastic strips that lined the bottoms of the screens, they proved no obstacle to cockroaches, or to the smaller mice. And so it was that before long, the library had become the permanent residence of a good many *chingchoks*, cockroaches, and mice.

Thotsakan had always hated bug spray. When he was a young man, and had few possessions to protect, he had been willing to scratch his mosquito bites, and in fact did so for upwards of ten years. When he married and had a son, he set himself up as something of an expert lecturer on the evils of DDT, both its immediate danger to the user and its long-term effects. But when he had amassed a good number of books, and when their enemies had begun to increase in number to an alarming degree, given an apparent lack of dependable birth control measures, Thotsakan was forced to resort to the weapons nearest to hand, however he might dislike them. First, he tried the little cans of glue that sell for thirty-five baht apiece. Indeed, the mice would stick to the baited glue. Unfortunately, it was not unusual for a *chingchok* to meet his fate there as well, and getting the too-often still kicking mice and frantically squirming *chingchoks* off the glue in order to kill and dispose of them was not at all a pleasant task. It was especially difficult, he found, to get a *chingchok* unstuck without ripping off some body parts. As for the mice, they either had to be beaten to death or drowned, and by the time the mouse had succumbed, the executioner himself was usually near to fainting. All of this became a frequent family activity.

As far as one could tell, the *chingchok* troops did not lay eggs in any great number, but there were a good many bellies in production, and however many tactics Thotsakan employed, the little monsters were never entirely defeated. As for the infant *chingchoks*, although they were far less able to defend themselves, they were more likely to escape execution. One day, after Thotsakan had sat for awhile, staring morosely at a herd of infant *chingchoks* scurrying playfully into and out of the cracks between his books, he went to his wife in high dudgeon.

"Woy! What am I to do? *Chingchok* shit all over my books! I swear to you, I'm going to kill them all."

"Why don't you, then, instead of coming to complain to me?" Sida was becoming irritated. It was bad enough, when a husband pulled a long face; in Thotsakan's case, a wife had to endure ten long faces! He stared mopishly at his wife, who was only too familiar with his tendency to bear grudges. But then, his gaze shifted to his son, and his anger melted away.

WHEN HANUMAN WAS BORN . . .

Thotsakan could scarcely believe his eyes when he first saw the son of his blood. He was staggered at the sight of Hanuman, for he had never imagined that the son of a demon, a robust demon at that, would be so tiny—and Thotsakan's new son was a very tiny baby indeed. His skin was yellow, which after a few days gave way to a deep bluish-green; his skin was dry, and wrinkled. Thotsakan was numb with shock, all but paralyzed by the unbelievable but undeniable fact that had been put before his eyes. The doctor told Thotsakan that there was something wrong with Hanuman's heart. It was no one's fault; no one could explain why such things happened—perhaps the astrologers, the sympathetic doctor had added with a sad shrug.

And his Sida, his dear Sida, lay motionless, with liquids dripping from a tube into her arm. It was many days before she was able to see her son. Meanwhile, there was only Thotsakan to watch the tiny body being warmed inside the incubator, inside the room made of glass, inside the hospital. There, he met many fathers and mothers who also had come to visit their infants. Most of them just stood and stared at the little open mouths that cried soundlessly on the other side of the glass. Thotsakan looked at other babies, some in worse condition than his son. The realization that he suddenly had new friends, people who shared the same fate, slowly dawned upon him, along with the realization that it was a club of which no one had ever wanted to be a member.

One afternoon, as he stood looking through the glass into the room that was safe from germs, Thotsakan noticed that a man about his own age was leaning against the glass, his forehead against his arm, his other hand in his pocket. From the look in his eyes, Thotsakan could see that the man was watching some scene in his imagination, far from the reality that lay before him: twin girls, lying upon their sides, neither of whom could have weighed more than 1,500 grams. Their eyes were half-closed, their skin was ashen, and their bellies pulsed with each respiration; they were even wrinklier than the other babies, and it seemed as if their blood must have no color at all. Because they were twins, the visitors gravitated toward them, and began to make remarks.

"Will you look at them?" one woman said. "I ask you, what kind of terrible karma is that? In my next life, whenever it may be, may I not give birth to children such as these."

"Pitiful," another woman added.

As the young man turned away from the window, Thotsakan saw that his eyes were red. He pulled out a handkerchief and, after making a show of wiping perspiration from his forehead, he quickly wiped his eyes, cleared his throat, and said, "Those are my . . . sister-in-law's children."

For a moment, Thotsakan wanted to slap the man's cowardly face, but in the next moment he wanted to put an arm around his shoulder, give him comfort, and take comfort in return. However, instead of doing either of those things, he returned to watching his son through the glass.

Time passed, and doctors who had gone abroad to learn about such things took good care of Hanuman; they gave him medicines, and performed operations. The bodily suffering of the son, and the heartache of the mother and father, made them as one. When the child cried, the parents hurt. When the child was silent, the parents were frightened. If they could have, they would have taken every bit of his pain as their own.

Thotsakan, so tough-hearted in the past, became Thotsakan the soft-hearted, just like every other parent of a handicapped child. Yes, the demon king is soft-hearted, even with small, defenseless animals—even with newborn *chingchoks* on the walls of his precious library—when he thinks of a tiny baby in a glass box, in a glass room.

Now that we know these things, let us return to the war against the *chingchoks* . . .

Time has passed, and each *chingchok* who had evaded death as an infant has gone on courageously to propagate the race by producing tens of new *chingchoks*. Thotsakan continues to give the infants a chance, but he is relentless in pursuit of the agile adults, whom he chases with his weapon of choice: the plastic fly swatter. He goes to battle huffing and puffing, forgetting himself entirely when he spies them on the binding of a favorite book, or attempting to slink into the narrow spaces between the floorboards. Occasionally, however, he takes time out to open a screen, and gently brush a baby along the wall toward it—even though the effect of his kindness, too often, is to recruit a new member or two, despite his intentions. And nothing frustrates Thotsakan more than those infants who obstinately refuse to leave the place of their birth, though the ruler of the land has not only decreed their exile, but gently helped to promote it. Still, he lets them live, and so the library remains filled with juvenile *chingchoks*, waiting to grow up.

Hanuman is growing up, too. If he is not so robust as his papa, neither is he crippled. He is a clever boy, and a trickster like his father, which makes his mother love him all the more. Hanuman has seen his father rage at the *chingchoks* for so long that it seems normal to him. He once took it upon himself to go into the library, armed with rubber bands and backed by his monkey troops, and lay waste the little monsters once and for all. Thotsakan put an immediate stop to it, saying that there was no telling what damage might be done to the shelves and the books by such a mighty invasion. But Sida knew the secret in her husband's heart: some of the little creatures would no doubt fall like clumsy miniature crocodiles before the monkey troops, and among them might be some little *chingchok* who had had the misfortune to be born with a malformed heart.

Sida had told Thotsakan that she was willing to be the hard-hearted one, that the *chingchoks* had abused their privileges of residence long enough, and did not deserve to stay a day longer. Why, even the demon's own wife and son were not allowed into that room—except to clean it! As far as she was concerned, she had every right to declare war on the *chingchoks* herself. It must be said, however, that although Sida said these things she was not immune to the feelings her husband would not express. She knew what he was thinking, for she, too, had had thoughts of their son in his infancy, when she had looked at the tiny *chingchoks*. Nevertheless, she told herself firmly, the fact was that that matter had nothing to do with this matter.

Thotsakan rebuked Sida with the opinion that she was hard-hearted, and carried on to the effect that he couldn't understand why the female sex, once having decided either to be hard-hearted or soft-hearted, always had to go to extremes. Moreover, he had not given up, and would surely think of some successful plan to defeat the whole *chingchok* army and drive it out of his roomful of beloved treasures. As for Sida, she could not help but conclude, given the failure of several subsequent nonviolent measures, that perhaps the only thing left for Thotsakan to do was to learn Chingchokese, and attempt to negotiate.

One day, Sida realized that it had been a long time since her demon had complained about the *chingchoks* in his library.

"Thotsakan, have you come up with any new ideas lately about the *chingchoks*?"

"I do have an idea in mind, although I cannot be sure that it will work."

"And you've been keeping it a secret?"

"Not exactly." Thotsakan tenderly patted Sida's belly, which had been growing rounder for three or four months. "The truth is, I have decided that the best thing to do with *chingchoks* is—nothing. What I say is: to hell with *ching-choks*!"

And then the demon began to laugh, and Sida began to laugh with him, and the sound of their happiness resounded through seven heavens, found their son Hanuman and pulled him into the room, and the boy who was as a jewel in their sight began to laugh with the mother and father who loved him so dearly.

Thus it was that one day, the very last trace of the "spirit of the killer" quietly floated out of the heart of Thotsakan, King of the Demons, and disappeared forever.

(*Lalana* 2527/1984)

Thotsakan to the Garden

The monsoon rains had ended, the waters had long receded to leave the stilts of houses and the trunks of trees coated with rusty mud and dried weeds, and the soil had stiffened enough to be worked. True, the rotting residue of last year's garden remained, but new shoots were everywhere. Sida surveyed the scene with an expression of mild displeasure. She had put off this day for too long, with the excuse of other things to do.

Today was a holiday. After she finished her household chores, Sida descended into the garden, meaning to begin with the ditch in front of the house. The weeds there had already spilled thickly over the path; there was no time to lose. She sat down and began to cut away at them, shifting position from time to time to relieve the ache in her muscles. She tossed the weeds into the ditch. Eventually, she would fill this ditch, and have another plot of land to work with.

What a shame, really. The ditch into which she was busily tossing weeds once had been a pond filled with clear water. Their friends would come to sit beside it, and fish; one of them always brought his butterfly net. Thotsakan had brought water lilies home, both the blue and the yellow kind, and planted them himself because he was enamored of the colors. Many was the hour he had spent with his head beneath the surface of the water, his feet pointing at the sky as he poked the roots of his beloved water lilies into the bottom mud. *Anicha, anicha* . . . all is impermanence . . . Before long, the weeds had conquered the water lilies, which rotted and died. The general of the demons was exceedingly vexed, and promptly forgot all about them.

"Ah, what happiness we know!"

It was the general himself, making an appearing upon the porch, arrayed in a white shirt with a round collar and a pair of mustard-colored silky pants, an outfit that contrasted handsomely with his swarthy complexion. He shuffled forward in his clogs . . . *kraek-kraek-kraek*. Sida was glad to see him. Perhaps he would lend her a hand.

"You love it out there, don't you?" he called down to her. "Planting things in the dirt, cutting weeds . . ." The demon looked lovingly at his wife, a smile playing about his lips. "Do you see? When you love Thotsakan, you are not disappointed. Is it dirt and weeds you want? Well, you shall have them to your heart's content."

Sida flashed him a look from the corner of her eye, but said nothing. Thotsakan descended the stairs, watched her work for a few moments, then turned and shuffled back to the house. *Kraek-kraek-kraek*, went his clogs. "See you later, my dear."

"Why did you come out here?"

"To lend moral support," he responded, without turning around.

Sida grumbled to herself, "Chi! Cha! General of the demons, he carries on like a lord in a novel!" She laid her weed-cutting knife on the ground, and rested for a moment with her back against the trunk of the mango tree, feeling her hot mood abate along with the soreness in her limbs and back. A cool breeze blew from the rice fields behind the house. "What can one expect of him, after all? Just look at yesterday. . ."

Yesterday, even before he had washed his face Thotsakan had appeared in the kitchen doorway, leaning against the door jamb, to watch her wash dishes. He looked tired, though all he had done so far was to get out of bed.

"Oy! What a lot of work you have here. Do you want to hire someone to help out? Watching you, I feel quite distressed. You should be looking fresh and pretty from morning to evening. But look at you: 'Nothing to look at—and only one child . . .'" Thotsakan was very fond of this slogan, which he had adapted from a television commercial.[1] He grinned engagingly at her. Once he started this kind of talk, there was no stopping him. "Ah well, I'm sure it's no good, comparing women that way, no good at all . . . Still, to be scrupulously honest with you, the fact is that I don't like helping with housework."

1. In the actual commercial for beauty soap, the words are, "Look, the mother of all those children—and still, so lovely!"

Sida had had to hurry with the dishes, for steam had begun to rise from the tea kettle that stood beside the rice pot over the charcoal she had just stirred. In a moment, after she had finished washing the supper dishes, she would fill the thermos with hot water and start fixing the soup of salty fried meat and ivy gourd of which Thotsakan was extremely fond, and which with any luck would be done at the same time as the rice, and then . . .

A glance in her husband's direction told Sida that he was beginning to sulk. Well, her own mood was deteriorating, too, and despite herself she suddenly burst out, "I don't like to do all these things, you know, but I must do them! If you want me to sit around prettying myself up, why don't you take over in here? Would you like that? When you finish in the kitchen, it will be time to soak the laundry. Then we eat. Of course, at eight o'clock you'll have to run for the train to get to work on time."

Although the tone of his wife's voice suggested to the demon the image of a hand reaching out to twist his face, Thotsakan had to laugh in spite of himself. "All right! Pardon me, please, and calm yourself. Why don't we get a girl to help you, to save me from housework, and to make you prettier? Tell me the truth—wouldn't you like that? I want my wife to be prettier."

Sida began to calm down. "We don't have enough money at the end of the month even now," she said, in a nicer voice, but increasing the speed with which she moved about the kitchen, for fear that he would be late for work. He was offended by her response to his kind offer. His laughter faded abruptly, and the tone of his reply was like the sudden hiss of a vexed snake.

"Eh? This business of sewing at home—how much money is that bringing in, eh? How many *satang* come into this house from the dressmaking?[2] A lot of prattling, gossiping women—that's what comes into this house." So saying, Thotsakan sat down next to the basin of dishes, planting his bottom on the cement floor with perhaps more force than he had intended. "I only mean well, and wish the best for you. I see you tired from all this work, with no one to help you—and, as I have already explained, I—well, I cannot help you, and so you might think about getting one of the neighborhood girls—Old Lakshmi's daughter, or Uncle Ongkot's.[3] When Hanuman was a baby, didn't you hire them a time or two? You could get one of them in here now, to help with the sewing."

Sida thought about it. For a moment, she imagined herself floating . . . cloaked in the radiance of a first lady. And then, memories of the past invaded her reverie, of the days when she had been nothing but a helper in a dressmaking shop, the days before Thotsakan had come into her life. Ah, well, she had a good husband, it was true, and she had become a respectable matron, more or less.

Sida thought about Benchakai and Kaikesi, the neighbors' teenaged daughters, who were in and out of Sida's

2. A *satang* is equivalent to less than one U.S. cent.

3. In the *Ramakian*, Sida is a human incarnation of the (Hindu) goddess Lakshmi, and Prince Ram is the human incarnation of the god Narayan. Ongkot is the son of Thotsakan's consort, Nang Montho.

house nearly every day.[4] When Hanuman was a baby, and the girls were about twelve years old, Sida had occasionally hired them to babysit. Benchakai was rather a simple child. For all that she had to help care for her own two younger siblings, she had not a single trick with which to amuse Hanuman. She simply sat and watched him cry: his tears, snot, and sweat could have flooded the world, Sida thought, before Benchakai would move. Her ideas about child care were limited to two statements: "Hanuman, you want Big Sister to carry you?" and, "If you don't stop that, your mother will hit you." Other than that, she simply sat, chin propped on her hands, and stared at the TV screen.

There was one scene that Sida would never forget: Hanuman seated beside Benchakai in front of the TV, with a plate of mango slices and a bowl of pepper-and-salt between them. Benchakai sat slack-jawed and staring, as usual; but Hanuman was having a wonderful time, caked

---

4. In the *Ramakian*, Kaikesi is the mother of Prince Ram. Benchakai (or, Benyakai) is a demoness, the daughter of a character named Phiphek. Phiphek is the brother of Thotsakan, exiled for what Thotsakan sees as his disloyalty in interpreting one of Thotsakan's disturbing dreams as a sign that Thotsakan must return Sida to Prince Ram. Benchakai is forced by her uncle, Thotsakan, to magically assume the form of Sida, and appear on a riverbank before Prince Ram and his retinue, appearing to be deceased so that Ram will give up his campaign. Hanuman, however, is not fooled by this ruse, and builds a funeral pyre from which Benchakai springs, quite alive and in her true demonic form. The characters who bear these names in Sri Daoruang's story have no actual relationship to the characters in the *Ramakian*; she is simply using the names.

with mango, pepper and salt, from his crusted ears down to his sticky little feet.

As for Kaikesi, she was a fairly clever girl, and although she was an only child she had understood how to play with Hanuman and keep him happy. Kaikesi's chief fault was that she was easily bored. Sida had attempted to teach her to sew once before, in exchange for babysitting, but after three days Kaikesi had fled, bored beyond endurance.

Such were Sida's thoughts, on the day before the morning she finally went to work in her weedy garden.

When Thotsakan appeared on the porch again, he was dressed to go out. He peered down at Sida, who was now crouched beside the great earthen water jar, sharpening her weeding knife. "Sida! I'm going to look for old books at Sanam Luang.[5] If I see a nice tree that isn't too large to carry, I'll bring it home."

Sida nodded. "Good," she thought, as she watched him go off through the gate. "With him at Sanam Luang, I just might be able to get this whole area weeded today." She bent to her task once more, and soon was lost in day-dreams. She thought she would raise the edge of this ditch, yes, make it quite high, and then she would divide the orange lilies and Japanese lantern flowers that now grew clustered around the base of the mango tree, and replant them there. When they bloomed, they would make a lovely show of reds and oranges. And over there,

5. Sanam Luang is a park near the Grand Palace. It has been used for royal ceremonies of various kinds, including royal cremations. At the time this story was written, it was also the site of the huge Weekend Market, which is now located at Chatuchak Park.

she thought, looking off into the distance, she would plant cosmos, in all three colors.

Not an hour had passed when she heard Thotsakan's voice. He stood in front of the house with a small bag of candy in his hand. She got up, went to him and said, "You can't have gone to Sanam Luang and back in an hour."

"The train was late and the buses are too damned slow. I've quite lost the book-buying feeling—and so, I thought I would come home and help my wife in the garden."

Sida was dumbfounded. She took the small bag of candy from his hand, and he went upstairs to change his clothes. Thotsakan was a demon of many moods, she thought, and they were continually changing. But—this! Digging in the dirt? Cutting weeds? Could it be that the general was going to the trenches?

And then, a few minutes later, whose boy was this, coming down the stairs in his shorts? Thotsakan strode forward, hitching his beloved, ragged cut-off jeans all the way up to his navel and knotting a *phakhaoma* firmly about his waist.

"You'll need another *phakhaoma*, for your head," Sida said. "I'll go get it." When she returned, he wrapped it turban-like about his head, to keep the sun off.

"Well, where's the hoe?"

Sida put her hands on her hips, smiling as she surveyed the scene. So, this would not be the day she finished weeding the plot, or even dividing and replanting the bulbs. Still, she was not unhappy. Rather, she was curious to know how events would unfold. Her thoughts turned to the kitchen, and the lunch she would now have to prepare. And the snacks he would want with his beer later. But all she said was, "So, you're really going to do this?"

"You just tell me where you want the weeds cut, that's all."

Sida pointed, then returned to her bulbs, being careful to keep a safe distance from the blinding light cast by a toiling demon. He raised his hoe, and brought it crashing down with mighty strokes. Weeds were crushed, thrashed and scattered without mercy in the two square meters of the garden where she had set him to work. The demon's sweat poured down his body, and drenched the hair down the length of his powerful back. His face became red, his breathing labored.

"Er-r! This is fun! I'm quite enjoying myself, Sida. How would it be if I were here all the time, working beside you?" As he spoke, his eyes swept the landscape beyond their garden. But Sida scarcely noticed his distant gaze, so full was her heart, so pleased was she with her beloved demon.

"Do you mean it?"

"Of course I mean it." He pointed at another plot of ground nearby. "Now, do you want that plot turned over, too?"

Sida nodded. She could scarcely believe her eyes. Thotsakan was like an athlete, one who had warmed up, and now—"buk-buk-buk!"—the hoe, sharpened by long use, bit into the dirt savagely, descending to half its width. Again and again, he raised it high above his head, then brought it crashing down, thrashing the clods of earth with great force, causing showers of defeated dirt to rain upon his *phakhaoma*-covered head.

After awhile, the sweating demon lowered the hoe to the ground, and looked about him. "Hr-r . . . there's nobody out there."

"Nobody out there?"

"To see."

"To see what?" Sida was bewildered.

"Aow—to see me helping you! Where are all the 'woo-men libs' ?"[6]

"Aw-w . . . Isn't one woo-men enough?"

Thotsakan was getting irritable. "I'll tell you what's enough," he said. "This is enough!" With these words, he took aim, reached back, and hurled the hoe into the air. Without looking to see where it landed, he tore the *phakhaoma* from his head, shook off the dirt, and wiped his eyes. Immediately, Sida set about trying to please him, sensing a fearful mood approaching.

"Oh dear, you really mustn't do anymore. Why, if anyone did pass by, they would think what a terrible wife you have, torturing you out here. Why don't you go and bathe now, and—and you can go on with this another day."

Thotsakan quickly nodded, tossed the *phakhaoma* over his shoulder, and strode off to have his bath. Sida picked up the hoe, and stood holding it, looking somewhat regretfully at the lily bulbs that lay scattered about her. She would have to leave them, for now, and make lunch.

She had not yet lighted the charcoal when she heard the demon roar, "I'm off to Sanam Luang! What the hell kind of weeds are those, anyway? I'm itching all over!"

6. In the Thai text, this is a transliteration of the sound of the words "women's lib" (พวกวูเมนลิบส์).

Sida suppressed a grin. No matter what, Thotsakan, General of the Demons, King of Lanka, had made his royal procession to the battlefield, where he had subjugated the weeds, and returned—with blisters between his fingers.

(*Lalana* 2528/1985)

Thotsakan: Sick of War

It was a holiday . . .

Thotsakan was making an exception in not going off in search of old books—his usual holiday activity. This decision may have had something to do with its being almost the end of the month, or perhaps he was simply feeling enervated and didn't want to go anywhere. Or, perhaps because he was engrossed in a particularly good science fiction novel, he was uninterested in the doings of the world that lay before him.

He began the day in his library, dusting books. Then he turned on the tape recorder, and stood with an unlit cigarette in one hand, a cup of no longer hot tea in the

In the original text, the title of this story, *Songkhram rok*, is a pun. *Songkhram* means war. *Rok* means disease, while *lok* means world. The term *songkhram lok* is used to mean "World War" (i.e., "*war* of the world"); by substituting "l" for "r," Sri Daoruang creates the term "*sick* of the world."

other, and his favorite science fiction book wedged under an armpit, listening to jazz notes thrumming through the air. With an air of satisfaction, the general of the demons proceeded to a chair under the shade of a tree, dressed in his customary at-home attire.

The customary at-home attire of the demon consists of a checkered *phakhaoma*, beneath which he does not trouble himself to wear any "gentlemen's private matters."[1]

"Sida!" he called. "This tea of yours is cold. Could you bring me a cup of coffee?"

"Whatever you want. Just don't blame me when you're lying there tonight and can't sleep."

Thotsakan rose, and followed the sound of his wife's voice. He found her sitting beside the morinda tree, pulling weeds that had invaded the aloe vera. She did not look up, but went on with her task, surrounded by her weed basket and her spade, and a bucket of fertilizer. Sida had become very interested in medicinal herbs, lately, but flowers and vegetables continued to flourish in her garden. Three tidy rows of cabbage grew nearby, with cosmos and zinnia neatly planted between the rows. Thotsakan watched his wife, her small hands worn from such toil, first pull weeds, then hoist the bucket of steer manure, sprinkle it around the remaining, desired plants, work it into the soil with her trowel, and, finally, pour water where she had worked.

1. This was the slogan in an advertisement for men's underwear. Instead of referring to underwear per se, the advertisement politely referred to the garments as "a gentlemen's private matters" (*rueang suan tua khong phuchai*/เรื่องส่วนตัวของผู้ชาย)

The sound of jazz pouring from the window and filling the garden chased away the former ambiance, which had been provided by country songs emanating from Old Phrot's tape recorder, next door.[2]

Thotsakan, raising his voice to compete with the jazz trumpet, announced, "We have true happiness, don't you think? Though its floor may not be *pu-pake*,[3] our house is lovely, and it is our house."

Sida turned and smiled like a good wife.

"Well, isn't it so?" he continued. "We have flowers, we have trees, plenty of birds, butterflies everywhere; a ditch filled with morning glories and mimosa; a pond afloat with water lilies . . . such beauty, everywhere we look . . ."

The demon general murmured on in his happiness as he set his cup of cold tea on the ground beside Sida, and re-settled his bottom into the old bamboo chair beneath the shady tree. He closed his lips on a fresh cigarette, and prepared to enter the world of the science fiction novel he held in his hands. "I ask you, what more could a person want? I tell you—this is happiness."

Old Phrot appeared on the other side of the ditch, staggering slightly, his head tilted back as if he were admiring the sky. He peered at Thotsakan and Sida for a moment, then gave out a cough that shook his skinny frame.

2. In the *Ramakian*, Phrot is a half-brother of Prince Ram. The Thai reader understands that this character is an Indian living in Thailand.

3. The word *pu* means "to lay (a floor, rug, etc.); *pake* is a Thai transliteration of the French word "parquet." "Though our house may not have a fancy parquet floor . . ."

"Ahem . . . Khun Thotsakan, my good sir . . . When I see you in your happy state, I am indeed happy for you, heh heh . . ."

Old Phrot gave the general of the demons a more or less snappy salute, as was his custom. Thotsakan shook his head slowly, and exhaled a deep sigh. Truly, the demon had once rather liked Old Phrot. He had a good heart. In the evenings, if he heard the bang-bang of a hammer being struck in the direction of Thotsakan and Sida's house, he would be leaping over the ditch in the next moment, offering to lend a hand. But that was before he had descended to his current state, in which he seemed to get as drunk on a shot as on a bottle. Many years had passed since Somsong had fled, and Old Phrot had become a regular "Old Phak," so drunk from morning until night that he had lost his job as the official janitor at the amphoe offices.[4]

Thotsakan remained silent. When he saw Old Phrot turn away, his cheerful mood returned. "Sida, a woman who truly understands me, who truly loves me—let us say that one or two such women came to live with us. Would you mind? Of course, I would choose women less beautiful than you."

---

4. This is a reference to the main character in the 1981 national award-winning novel, *The Judgment*, by Chart Kobjitti, a close friend of Sri Daoruang and her husband. In the novel, a young villager named Phak descends into drunkenness as the result of his neighbors' cruel behavior after he decides to take in and care for his father's retarded young widow.

An *amphoe* is approximately equivalent to a county, or township. In Chart's novel, Phak is a janitor at the village school.

Sida was used to this kind of teasing from her demon general. He talked a lot, but she had yet to see any of these women appear. They were the stuff of dreams, these perfect creatures, drawn from the other worlds of his science fiction novels and from fairy tales of princes and princesses, the kind where a prince down on his luck happens to meet a demon princess, and so on, dreams not unlike those of other young men, and some not so young.[5] And she herself had equal rights insofar as dreaming was concerned, Sida thought . . . and thought . . . and smiled to herself, for her most recent interesting dream, were she to give it a number, would be somewhere in the hundreds. In this, she and her demon were alike.

Thotsakan smiled blissfully up at the small pink blossoms on a vine that climbed and clung to the branches of the mango tree, quite possibly considering how particularly beautiful blossoms are, when they are twined about the branches of an alien plant. "Er . . . Sida. I tell you, I think this tree may have its own feelings. Think about it. It is capable of growth, and also death; it reproduces, it even eats—fertilizer, and so on—so why should it not have feelings, too? Yes, I speak of the feelings of a tree—and don't misunderstand me, but I almost wish that you would never cut into their bodies. Perhaps they hurt, just as we do."

Sida wished to agree with these poetic words, but life interfered. "The weeds would be over your head," she said.

5. This is a reference to Prince Ram's encounter with the demoness Samanakha, Thotsakan's notoriously amorous sister (see chapter 2).

"I am talking about big trees," he said, "not weeds."

And then it happened . . . Like the coming of the monsoon, like crashes of thunder that split the sky—*priang! priang!* Something has come this way to kindle the demon's anger . . . And the something happens to take the form of Old Phrot's reddish-brown dog, which has sneaked onto the demon's property once again—no one knows how.

"Oh, no!" Sida cries, "Our dried beef! You must have left the door open again, husband!"

The general of the demons is stupefied to see the dried, salted beef upon which he would have snacked while he drank his afternoon beer—his very own dried, salted beef!—dangling from the mouth of this—this general of the dogs! Thotsakan tosses aside his science fiction novel, jumps to his feet, seizes the spade, and is off in pursuit. He seems to fly through the air as he clears the ditch, his *phakhaoma* fluttering behind him . . . [6]

Old Phrot's dogged disciple is wily and fast. He disappears beneath his master's house, and in a flash is out the other side and all the way down the lane to the intersection where it meets the big road.

The angry demon, choking with rage, glares at Old Phrot, who by now has managed to clamber to his feet.

6. Sri Daoruang uses exactly the language of the *Ramakian*, here: *asura dot kham du dai muean ho* (อสุราโดดข้ามดูได้เหมือนเทาะ). *Asura* is one of the several words meaning "demon"; *ho* means to fly—but only supernatural beings, demons, and "superheroes" *ho*; airplanes and birds *bin*, fly.

Thotsakan raises the spade high above his head, brings it crashing down onto an old metal laundry basin which lies overturned beneath the house, and makes his declaration of war:

"This is how you raise your dog? To cause trouble for your neighbors?" He picks up the spade again, holds it inches from Old Phrot's face, and shouts, "I'm telling you, from now on I'm going to poison every dog that jumps the ditch! And you—you can stop pretending to be drunker than you are when you come over to borrow money, you old fraud!"

Sida stood with trembling heart. She could scarcely imagine that a "dog war" would become a "people war," or that limited warfare could so quickly escalate into a global confrontation, enveloping her demon in its dark heat, and destroying his peaceful contemplation of their lovely garden. True, his anger was excessive, given the situation. What would be the best thing to do? Go to the kitchen, yes, that was it—and fix something to soothe him; and so she hurried off.

His moods were so changeable, she thought, beginning to feel rather irked. The week before, Sida had asked him to remove some vines growing on the mango tree, not the pretty ones but parasites that would do the tree harm, in time, and he had made so many excuses that Sida had finally grown vexed, and said that she would climb the tree herself. Thotsakan had scowled, hitched up his precariously knotted *phakhaoma*, grabbed a knife, and scurried up the trunk of the tree at once. Sida had fled into the house, expecting to be embarrassed before the whole neighborhood, but fortunately there was no breeze, and it appeared that the demon general had passed his exams in the monkey sciences. Eventually he had appeared before her, showing off the scratches on his ribs, and humming the tune, "The Scars of a Hundred Old Wounds."

Sida spread a mat beneath the mango tree in which the flowers climbed, and set down a tray containing a dish of crispy fish salad and a bottle of beer. The demon, with less fire in his eye now, but also without the cheerful sparkle with which he had greeted her earlier, came and sat crosslegged on the mat, and accepted the cold bottle of Amarit that she held out to him.

Sida said, "Truly, I myself was careless; I must have been dreaming not to put the dried beef in a high, safe place. Still, I must say that you should not have gone to your neighbor's house to hit his dog."

Thotsakan muttered, "To tell you the truth, I don't even recall running over there . . . I myself admit that this sort of behavior is not correct."

The two of them sat and looked in the direction of Old Phrot's house. He was nowhere to be seen. Thotsakan and Sida began to speak of one thing and another, of new dreams and old ones. The subjects of their two-track conversation merged at points, and diverged at others. They expressed both reasonable thoughts and seemingly senseless ones, and various combinations of both; in short, it was the sort of conversation two people often have when they are alone together, and have been married for a long time.

Hanuman had gone to an afternoon movie, which lent a certain freedom to their speech.

"As a matter of fact, I do not care for violence," Thotsakan declared. "If you give me a choice of films—one about war and the other about sex, I'll take sex every time."

"Tomorrow," Sida said, "we really must go to market, and get some charcoal. We're almost out."

Thotsakan smiled. "If I'd have caught the little sonofabitch, I'd have killed him with my bare hands—I could have done it, you know."

Sida laughed. "You're very strange."

"But lovable, eh? If I just had Nang Montho here beside me, too . . . Just one more, I think I could do with one more, and—" But Thotsakan never finished his sentence, for at that moment he espied a group of young boys hopping across the ditch into his garden. In their hands, they carried slingshots; the young hunters' eyes were fixed on the *tabaek* tree. At first, the sight of them reminded Thotsakan of the happy days of his own boyhood, and then—suddenly, he leapt to his feet and began running toward them.

"Boys! Boys! Don't do it! Birds are alive, just like us. Anyway, those birds are so little, they wouldn't make a meal for one of you."

The boys hadn't heard his words in time. Their weapons had already fired—*plua! plua!*—toward one small target, a black and white magpie that had been preening itself, and now plunged into the tall weeds. The boys leaped up, shouting with joy, then scrambled forward and wrestled with each other amongst the weeds over their prey, which at last lay fluttering feebly in the open hand of their leader.

Thotsakan's beard shuddered with the effort of suppressing his rage, but he was determined to speak to them in a pleasant manner.

"Boys, come here . . . Let Uncle buy it from you, eh? How many baht do you want?"

But the boys' pride in their achievement far outweighed their desire for a few baht. They argued together over which of them was, in fact, the "*naksu phu phichit*," and threw contemptuous glances in Thotsakan's direction as they made off with their prize.[7]

"Get out!" he screamed. "I don't want to see any of you on my property again, do you hear me? Not for killing birds, not for anything. Get out, you little bastards! And tell your fathers what I said!"

Old Phrot, who had been napping on his porch, sprang up confusedly and looked all around. The lovely Sida felt very upset as she watched the boys leap the ditch, almost missing their footing on the other side and falling in. The general of the demons lifted the spade above his head and, striking a mighty pose, plunged it into the soil. No mistake, this was a declaration of war!

Thotsakan's wrath filled the earth, and Sida was frightened. The science fiction novel had been tossed aside. The mood of cheerful contemplation had vanished utterly, the pleasant, teasing conversation of only a few moments

---

7. A virtually untranslatable term, *naksu phu phichit* (นักสู้ผู้พิชิต) refers to fighters in a Chinese "action" film.

before was forgotten. Thotsakan lifted his glass of Amarit to his lips, and drained it swiftly—*ugg-ugg-ugg*. His castle of dreams had crumbled.[8] Nang Montho, that lovely creature, had been pushed out of heaven and come crashing to earth.

Thotsakan's mind had room only for rage, and thoughts of revenge, thoughts that were interrupted by the sound of fists pounding—*kroom kroom kroom*—on the rusty gate in front of the house.

"Uncle! Uncle! Open the gate!"

"What is this—more damned boys?!"

Sida ran toward the gate, spoke with them briefly, and ran back to her husband. "They aren't the same boys!" she said breathlessly. "These are different boys, from down at the intersection. They're after Ai Daeng, Old Phrot's dog. He bit a child, and—oh, look! There he is! Running toward the back of the house!"

Everyone looked in the direction Sida was pointing. Old Phrot shouted from his porch, "Get him! Get the sonofabitch and kill him—he's nothing but trouble. Whoever can kill him, do it and let that be the end of it!"

---

8. A direct translation of the term I have translated as "castle of dreams" would be, "palace(s) for three seasons" (*prasat sam ruedu/* ปราสาทสามฤดู). This is a reference to the palaces promised to Prince Siddhartha, by his father, if only he would remain in his princely life instead of going off to become a mendicant. Prince Siddhartha spurned his father's offer, and eventually achieved enlightenment, and became the Buddha. The term *prasat sam ruedu* is commonly used to imply riches, a beautiful home, and the good life, or "a castle of dreams."

Five or six great lads entered the garden, all regulars in the neighborhood tinner gang, all armed with sticks and clubs, wild in their eagerness, their eyes scanning the horizon.[9] In the next moment, everyone saw Ai Daeng streaking behind the house, a sight which almost caused Sida to laugh in spite of herself, for Thotsakan's jazz tape provided the perfect soundtrack for this solo dog race. She stepped aside, thinking that the neighborhood glue-sniffing gang would soon assuage her demon's rage at Ai Daeng, who had now made a name for himself as an indiscriminate biter. But the troops never had a chance to mobilize, for they found themselves face to face with the general of the demons, one hand on his hip, the other hand making a wide sweep before him as he made a pronouncement that "challenged the sky, dared the earth . . ."[10]

"All of you—out of here! I have made a decision: whether Ai Daeng is a mad dog or a good dog—whether a creature is a bird, or a person, or any other kind of animal, if it comes here seeking sanctuary, it will be safe. No one can make Thotsakan's garden into a battlefield."

At the end of this declaration, everyone was silent. No one dared to speak a word of protest. The tinner gang turned with their sticks and clubs in their hands and filed through the gate, staring backwards all the while at Thotsakan, with dazed looks on their faces. Old Phrot was

9. "Tinner" is "thinner," the paint thinner sometimes sniffed by slum kids, and other kids in Thailand. It is called "tinner" because there is no "th" in Thai.

10. The name of a song that was very popular at the time this story was written.

hanging onto the railing of his porch with one hand, to keep from falling off, and rubbing his eyes with the other.

Fed up, Sida turned and went into the house. She didn't care any more. In an instant, the situation had reversed itself completely!

As for the general of the demons, he had to lie down for a while, and utter many long, deep sighs.

Time passed, along with many bottles of Amarit beer . . .

Thotsakan was not a happy demon. When it was time to eat, he didn't want to eat. When it was time to sleep, he wasn't tired. He had even become irregular, as the result of stress. His stomach was a dark and roiling pit in his midsection. When he did lie down, his head spun. He had a recurring nightmare in which a gang of boys amused themselves by throwing a magpie back and forth, before letting it drop and then wrestling for it. Their sneery attitude, the way they rudely raised their eyebrows at the demon made him so angry that he picked up a spade and chased them with it. But he never reached the murderers in time because the tinner gang, carrying huge pliers, got in his way.

At last, Thotsakan developed an ulcer.

One afternoon, as the demon lay moping, Sida appeared as usual, bearing a tray of refreshments. But—what was this? Instead of the bottle of beer he expected, the tray was covered with an array of strange-looking potions and pills.

"I made these things myself, from our own garden," she announced proudly, and a bit nervously. "See? Sweet-smelling little pills made of turmeric and honey; they'll be good for your ulcer. And here," she said, pointing at little mounds of pale shreds and powders, "are lime, and aloe vera, for your headache." Before he could comment, she quickly added, "First, we'll dab a bit of lime on each temple, and then a bit of aloe vera. After that, you drink some nice tea I made from a creeper on the mango tree— not the one with the pretty flowers, another one. And no more coffee! When you drink this tea instead, you'll have nicer dreams. If that doesn't work, I will boil up some cassia leaves with spirits, one dose to sleep and another dose to prevent nightmares. And then—"Enough!" Thotsakan cried out, sinking back against his pillow.

Despite her cheery and determined demeanor, Sida hadn't been at all sure how she was going to get these remedies down him, when he had balked at taking even the little foreign pills that didn't have any smell. The pills she had made with turmeric and honey had a sweet scent, and so did the tea she had made from the leaves of the creeper. She had hoped they would tempt him . . . All she could do was to try.

The general of the demons cast a lugubrious eye over the remedies she had brought him. "Oy, take it all away," he moaned. "All right, I promise—no more dreams! And if I do dream . . . I swear . . . I will dream only of my dear mother!"

(*Lalana* 2528/1985)

Sida Puts Out the Fire

"Sida, I'll be late tonight."

Truly, Sida had been preparing herself to hear these words from him. The only thing she had not been able to guess was the exact nature of the ruse he would employ. She cast a glance at her beloved demon, and her heart pounded. She tried to suppress the feelings that surged within her, to speak in a perfectly normal tone of voice, for she herself had a thing or two to conceal, and thus had to lower her head and avoid his eyes as she asked, "Will you be home in time for dinner?"

"Probably not. A friend invited me out. You and the boy had better go ahead and eat. No need to wait for me."

When it came to loving and deeply caring for one's wife and child, Thotsakan was in a class by himself. Not once had he come home in the dark of night with no explanation for his behavior. And before going out the door each morning, he would always hug his wife and give her a smacking kiss on the cheek.

Today was no exception. He called out to his son, "Hey, Hanuman, Papa's boy—whose mama am I kissing here, eh?"

The son was like the father. At his papa's words, he came tumbling onto the scene like an actor in a Chinese movie, landing between his parents in the attitude of a Ninja set to strike. Sida got up and left the jokesters to their tricks. Those two! As usual, the moment they perceived that no one was admiring their performance, it ended. Thotsakan sent Hanuman out to buy him a pack of cigarettes, and hurried into the bathroom to finish getting ready.

While her husband bathed, Sida was able to quell the heat in her heart sufficiently to be sure that her voice would not tremble, and that the tears would stay in her eyes where they belonged. "I must not seem any different from usual."

She forced herself to smile when her beloved husband emerged fully dressed from the bathroom, and even to tease him.

"My, how handsome you look," she said with a sweet smile. But she was unable to resist adding, "This 'friend' wouldn't happen to be a woman friend, would it?"

"An m-a-n friend," he replied, drawing out the letters as he picked up his shoes. He carried his shoes from the bedroom, and then returned to the bathroom once again. He shook a little cologne over his hair, patted some on his throat, and then reached inside his shirt and dabbed some into his armpits. He combed his hair again, and also his moustache. "Why do you ask?"

"I don't know."

"Do you suspect something, is that it?"

"No."

He smiled at her reflection in the mirror. "Thotsakan is old, my dear. Nobody wants him. Uh, where's that little comb I keep in my pants pocket? Did you wash it? If you wouldn't mind finding it for me . . ."

"Here it is."

"Ah." He planted a light kiss on Sida's forehead and, taking the comb from her hand and the pack of cigarettes from Hanuman's, went swaggering off down the path with a cigarette stuck in his mouth. And then, just as he did every day, Thotsakan turned and looked back at his wife and child.

Never, since they had begun to share their lives with each other, had there been a hint that Thotsakan might have other women. If it was true . . . if this, the thing that she suspected, turned out to be true, never again would his word be sacred to her. He had caused Sida to feel a great, heavy, sorrowful anger. Had he no shame, before her and their son? (Was Thotsakan not only ten-faced, but two-faced as well?)

Very early this morning, while it was still dark, and she had been removing things from the demon's pants pockets in order to lay out a fresh outfit for him to wear that day, she had pulled out his black pocket comb, his keys, his wallet, and his notebook, and set them before the mirror. She pulled out a handkerchief and tossed it into the hamper.

And then, something unusual happened. Sida turned and looked this way and that, to be sure that she was alone and then she was seized with the desire to pick up the little

83

black notebook . . . and open it . . . and read it. Something, some kind of a gossipy voice seemed to be talking inside her head, and it was saying pick up the notebook, pick it up, read the notebook, and a feeling stole from her heart out to her finger-tips, an irresistible feeling that caused her to reach out, snatch up the notebook, and read every single page in the "daily diary" part.

On those narrow pages, her husband had written the telephone numbers of many people. Sida felt proud when she saw that her birthday and their son's birthday were written on the very first page. The dates of various events were jotted down, along with clever remarks that Thotsakan had thought of, or heard.

Sida came to the last jotting in the notebook, Thotsakan's notes for today, the fourteenth of October: "Birthday—Montho."[1] Eh—what was this?

October the fourteenth, oh marvelous day . . .[2] Thotsakan is going out, even though he doesn't have to go to work today. One of his "friends" is taking him out . . . he says. Now, Sida has no doubt of the true situation!

1. In the *Ramakian*, Montho is the queen and chief consort of Thotsakan.

2. The choice of October 14 has considerable significance for all Thais. As mentioned in chapter 1, this was the day, in the year 1973, when army and police troops attacked pro-democracy demonstrators, most of whom were university students, in the streets of Bangkok. This was also the day Suchat and Wanna Sawatsri (Sri Daoruang), who were deeply involved in these events, chose to be married in the following year, 1974. Thus October 14 is, for the author, a day of both calamity and celebration.

At that moment, the god of the wind sent a gust through the open window, and Sida ran to close the shutters, to keep the dust of the fields out of her home. She sank wearily onto her bed, and lay stretched out, face down in the gloom. The good Saturday TV movies that Thotsakan and his son loved would be watched by only one, today. Sida behaved like the worst of mothers, one who has no interest in her child, who does not bother to amuse him. She felt irritated by the stupid roar of the soap commercial coming from the other room, which had never bothered her before.

As the day progressed, Hanuman himself wondered what was going on, because on most Saturdays, he and his father would lie side by side watching TV, and his mother would bring them nice things to eat. But today she was quiet, and stayed in her room. She hadn't taken their dirty clothes out to soak in the basin yet, and there was a big pile of dirty cups, dishes, bowls, pots, and pans in the kitchen. Worse, she had actually yelled at Hanuman to go in there and wash them himself, as soon as "Yot Khon Daen Thuean" was over.[3]

Sida sobbed miserably, silently into her pillow. The flames of her hurt and anger billowed and subsided, fanned by awful thoughts that she could not suppress. What sort of creature did she seem, to him? Oh, she knew all too well that she had no "family" (and no birthmark,

3. This was the Thai title (ยอดคนแดนเถื่อน) given to the American film, "A Man Called Horse."

either).[4] Or perhaps he was simply bored with her. Had she done anything wrong? She was forced to admit that she would have been spared these dreadful thoughts and suspicions, had she not discovered his secret by sneaking into his diary—a thing a truly good wife would never have done.

From the first moment of their life together until today, nothing in his behavior had hinted of anything but love for her and for their child. Sida was sure that this woman he had found must be beautiful—in the way women who worked out in the world were beautiful. In fact, she was probably—oh, no! She was probably—an intellectual! And what was she, Sida, by comparison? A plain old up-country factory worker, that's what! The kind of woman who washes her face and combs her hair once a day, may-be twice, a woman whose clothes have never known the heat of an iron, a woman who never, during the course of a whole day, gives one thought to "two-way powder, 280 baht a box!"[5]

No, all Sida thought about was housework! She even thought that it was important; that, and helping her husband by making a little money here and there with her sewing, all of which somehow made the time disappear, day by day, almost without her knowing how, until she

4. This is another reference (see "Thotsakan and Sida") to the birthmark that proves the aristocratic origins of beleaguered heroines in Thai romance novels.

5. A phrase taken from a popular magazine advertisement. Sri Daoruang writes this partially in Thai, and partially in transliterated English words: *thu-wei phaodoe talap la 280* (ทู-เวย์-เพาเดอร์ ตลับละ 280).

could not help but wonder how so much time had gone by so swiftly, without her having accomplished much of anything worthwhile.

However, the hell with all that.[6] Now is what matters, Sida thinks dazedly. What is he doing now? Where is he doing it? (And how, exactly?) He is in a room somewhere with this woman, and they are alone. A voluptuous scene unfolds in Sida's mind, a scene that cannot but end with Thotsakan passionately embracing . . . her . . . what's-her-name—*E* Montho![7]

If the woman is so beautiful, if she is such an unforgettable lover . . . Oh, Hanuman, my poor little son, will you end up living with your papa, or your mama?

After lying in her tears for a long time, painting various pictures in her mind which can only deepen her sorrow and vexation, in Sida's mind there are only questions to which she cannot find answers. Exhausted from running in the frantic circles of her imagination, presently she begins to feel ashamed before her son, who has crept into her bedroom from time to time and then crept out again, terrified. She determines to rouse herself, and she does.

She goes to the bathroom, undresses, dips cool water from the earthen jar, and begins pouring it over her head. Dip and pour . . . dip and pour . . . the water streams down her body, and begins to wash away her sadness. Just

6. The Thai term that is used is *tae arai ko chang thoet* (แต่อะไร ก็ช่างเถิด). Although the word "hell" does not appear, the meaning of the phrase is nearly identical to "the hell with all that."

7. The preface *"E"* pushes Montho down to a low rung on the social ladder.

a little cool water pouring down from her head all over her body, and her tension, the giddy misery of her mind, begins to heal. Her skin feels clean and fresh, her thoughts are clearing, and the answers for which she had searched for so many unhappy hours begin to come.

"Aow! Aow! Come here, everybody, I'm home! Bearing gifts for both wife and son! Come and look!"

At about nine o'clock, Thotsakan's voice preceded him into the house. Hanuman sprang up, abandoning *Singha krai phop*.[8] He shouted, "Oh, ho-o, Mama—look at the beautiful cloth Papa brought for you! And candy for me— and a toy, too!" He turned quickly to his father, whispering, "I don't know what's wrong with Mama. She's been lying on her bed crying all day, and she even made Ninja Boy wash the dishes all by himself. It's been terrible here!"

Sida accepted her gift. Although she had firmly resolved the matter of how she would behave toward the source of her suffering, she was unable to muster the cheery smile she had planned. Thotsakan, however, was smiling from ear to ear; indeed, his face looked as jolly as a bowl of popped rice. There were two things about him that Sida could hardly fail to notice: first, he was as clean and fresh as the moment he had left the house that morning; and second, there was not one trace to be sniffed of the cologne that he had sprinkled over his hair, patted on his throat, and dabbed into his armpits.

"Do you want something to eat? Or perhaps you aren't —hungry, anymore . . ." She lightly shrugged off the arm

8. *Singha krai phop* (สิงห์ไกรภพ) was a televised version of a heroic epic tale written by the poet Sunthon Phu (1786–1856).

with which her beloved husband would have encircled her, a gesture in which he could not but discern a trace of disgust.

"I've eaten," he replied.

"I see. You don't seem to have had anything to drink at all—how odd. You and your friend get together, and you don't have a drink?"

There was something in Sida's tone of voice, and in the studied blankness of her expression, that pushed Thotsakan to the edge of his endurance. "What is this? Do you suspect me of something?"

"No." She lifted her chin, and sniffed. "How nice. You've had your bath. Now you won't have to argue with your son about who gets to bathe first." She turned to Hanuman. "Along with you, Hanuman, or did you plan to go to bed just as dirty as you are?"

Hanuman stood transfixed, his glance darting between his mother's face and his father's. He grinned nervously. "Papa, you should take a bath before you come home all the time—then we wouldn't be wasting so much water, right?" He was desperate to coax a laugh from his papa, but Thotsakan was not amused. In fact, his formerly cheerful face was fast clouding over with anger, and he no longer resembled a jolly bowl of popped rice. He was as silent as a grain of rice that refuses to pop, one that lies beside the fire like a pebble. He stalked out the front door, and sat down on the porch by himself, taking sulky drags on his cigarette. It was what he did whenever he felt resentful at having been criticized, or picked on. Sida followed a moment later, and sat beside him.

"What is this?" he asked angrily, glaring at her. "Can't I even go out to enjoy myself with my friends after working all week?"

"Absolutely. We all have the same rights, don't we?"

"And what is that supposed to mean? You want to go out? Aaw . . . So, my little Sida is capable of jealousy, after all."

"So, my demon admits that there is something to be jealous of? Yes, we all have the same "rights"—but some of us choose not to exercise them. I never told you not to go out with your friends. I'm not angry about that—I'm angry because you lied to me."

"I lied to you?"

"I read it in your notebook."

He could not believe it. Never would he have imagined that his beloved Sida, she with the honest face, would have thought of doing such a thing! Thotsakan's face turned such a deep shade of red that he began to look like Kuan U.[9] Suddenly he rose, picked up a chair, and slammed it down on the floor of the porch.

Hanuman heard the crash. He had been watching TV inside, and listening to the argument with half an ear. Now, he crept to a good vantage point from which to view the much more interesting proceedings outside.

"You are blaming me! So, my friend and I went to a massage parlor—so what? I hurry home from the massage

9. Kuan U was a faithful and brave general in the Chinese epic, *Three Kingdoms*, one of the first foreign books to be translated into Thai.

parlor, to my wife and child.[10] I even stop to buy gifts for my wife and child—and what do I find? A spy in my house, that's what I find. What I want to know is why I am now living with a spy in my house!"

Sida had expected Thotsakan to be silent because he was not only the guilty party but had been caught. She had not been prepared for the possibility that the tables might be turned, that she might be found to be the guilty party.

"Well, I know that I was wrong about that, I shouldn't have looked. Say what you like, curse me if you want to about that, and I won't argue. But I beg your indulgence to say that I never thought you would lie to me."

"So, you admit that you were wrong, and now—now what do you want from me? I'd have been better off not to come home at all."

"I'm not finished. I've said everything I have to say about you, but not everything I have to say about myself. From now on, I will never look at your notebook again, never."

"Hoy! How will I know? Such behavior, such a thing in my house—a spy in my house! I don't like it a bit. No matter what I do, I shall feel that I have no freedom in this life!"

Sida struggled to keep her voice down, to keep this conversation from growing into a shouting match—for she, too, was becoming angrier.

10. The author is making clear that until quite recently, in Thai society, a trip to the massage parlor with friends was not considered by either husband or wife to be in the same category of behavior as a lasting love affair with one person. The former occurrence would have little effect on the family; the latter might imperil or destroy it.

"Thotsakan, since the day we began with each other, have you ever caught me lying to you?"

"Have I ever caught you? Hah! Not you! Not the most perfect woman in the world! If you hadn't been, would I have chosen you to be Hanuman's mother? But now, now you are so much more than that—not only Hanuman's mother, but my mother, too!"

"You needn't be sarcastic. You will see. You can make all the notes you like on all your love affairs—whoever you have them with, and wherever you choose to conduct them, for all I care. Go on and fill your notebook with them, and see. Or maybe I will not be so successful. Maybe I will give in to temptation, and open the notebook again—maybe I will be no better at keeping my word than my husband is."

By now, Thotsakan had forgotten that it was he who had first stood accused. He ranted on until Hanuman grew so bored with hearing the words "a spy in my house" that he took himself off to bed. It was Sida, Thotsakan continued to insist, who had caused all of this trouble, with her admission to being a spy in his house. But, she continued to argue back, he had lied to her!

And so it went, on and on.

Since that unhappy day, Sida has felt quite proud of the way she conducted herself in the matter, and of the way in which she was able, finally, to gain control of her feelings. For in the end, she did. The "Nang Montho fire" has been extinguished—for the most part, although she is not altogether sure how she feels about some things. For example, if a husband comes to a wife in all honesty to announce what she had only suspected when she looked into his notebook, will that wife be grateful for his integrity? (Ah, now that is a question, is it not?)

Sida continues to believe in the importance of expressing one's feelings. It is a matter of self-respect, as far as she is concerned, both for herself and for her demon, and also a demonstration of both intimacy and sincerity. Such behavior ought to engender love and happiness between them, anew, if only because it will remind them that human beings are an imperfect lot, full of defects and weaknesses.

Today, Sida is able to touch the little notebook, the tempting object that caused so much trouble, with a sensation of victory, even though she still does not know whether she trusts her demon completely (or whether, for that matter, he trusts her). She has thought long and hard about the matter, and decided upon what she does know to be absolutely true: her demon loves and trusts her, no more and no less than she loves and trusts him; and there is no doubt that he is able to love her the more, because she was able to put out the "fire" that had consumed her on that terrible Saturday, the fourteenth of October.

Now, she is able to take his "things" from his pockets, and pile them in front of the mirror. And leave them alone.

Does he lie to her face, or behind her back? Either way, it is no responsibility of hers. She knows that she still loves him, and that his love for her has not waned. And she laughs to herself, when she remembers how Thotsakan, the picture of wounded self-righteousness, had announced, "I hurry home from the massage parlor, to my wife and child—I even stop to buy gifts for my wife and child!"

Wait and see. Another day, "Nang Montho" just may pay a call. Who can tell?

(*Lalana* 2528/1985)

Phaya Khon Possessed

This story happened once upon a time, long ago, before the *nok chan* had become a proper porch.[1] In those days, no matter if his house was old and beginning to fall apart, Thotsakan loved it, and the *nok chan* was the part he loved best.

On this evening, the demon general was there, sitting on a floor mat and leaning sideways against one of the fancy new triangular pillows he had bought, looking for all the world like some aristocratic lover in an old tale. He gazed at the sky, where the sun was about to set, reaching from time to time for one of the tasty morsels that Sida had provided, both hot and cold varieties.

Every so often, he would twist himself into a new position, complaining of an ache in his back or his neck, trying in vain to get comfortable against the new pillow,

1. This reference is an "in-joke" for friends of the author, who would remember the passage from *nok chan*, the plain, open area outside the door in a typical Thai house, to a real, roofed porch.

because it was something to which he was not accustomed. Sida had come out onto the porch at sunset, bearing the tray of tasty morsels, both hot and cold varieties, because it was something to which she was very well accustomed. The demon was lost in dreams, as he so often was. The fields that stretched on for a good distance behind the house to the southwest had lain fallow for some time. The owner had let them go to grass instead of planting rice— to avoid paying the taxes, the neighbors surmised. The demon did not care why the fields lay fallow. He simply enjoyed watching the ripples and waves of the grasses in the evening breeze, as he dreamed the dreams that carried him far beyond the peaceful scene that lay before him.

"Sida, someday I would like to have a house on a hill in the middle of vast fields, so vast that you couldn't see beyond them, just like ones in *Chao phaendin*.[2] Remember? And I would build an arched bridge across a stream beside my house, and the water in the stream would be so clear that you could see a needlefish swimming in it."

The sun had set, and a cool breeze blew across the *nok chan*, from south to north. No doubt about it, these were kite winds and no other. Beneath the darkling sky now filled with stars, the general of the demons peered out into the universe, smiling and waving to creatures on distant stars; for he believed that the stars were celestial ladies, and that they waved back at him.

2. The Thai title of the American film, *Giant*, based on the novel by Edna Ferber.

Yes, ladies. Thotsakan believes that the stars are ladies, that they look at him, and that these ladies are . . . differently made, in certain ways, from his own wife Sida. Just how the celestial ladies are different from herself is a matter about which Sida has wondered. Are they triangular? Perhaps they are square, these celestial beauties, or even round.

"Today at Ram the Indian's house," she said, "they sold something on credit and bought five cows."[3]

As we have already learned, Sida has developed the ability to listen to her husband talk about his dreams while pursuing a completely different conversation. Sometimes they carry on two entirely different conversations simultaneously for an amazing length of time.

"I'd like ten little mousies," he said thoughtfully, "ten little *e nu*—or would it be more polite to call them *nang nu*—what do you think?"[4]

Hanuman, who had been sitting quietly between his parents, showed allegiance to his mother by bawling out, "Our papa! That's how he is, chi-i-i-ldren!" imitating the announcer of one of his favorite television programs, "Missed Appointment."

---

3. In the first story, "Thotsakan and Sida," Thotsakan had bought many household items on credit from the "Ramalaks" (merchants of Indian descent) to Sida's despair. In this story, too, many of the characters are Indian residents of Thailand.

4. The word *nu* (หนู) literally means "mouse." But *nu* also is used as a personal pronoun by a girl or woman who is younger than the person to whom she is speaking; that person may also use the word *nu* in speaking to her. Thotsakan, teasing his wife, is using *e nu* and *nang nu* (literally, "little sister") to mean, approximately "little cuties."

"Hm-m. Pretty little Apson told me they paid 10,000 baht apiece for them," Sida said.[5] She was sometimes successful in bringing him back to earthly conversation by employing such measures.

"Who? What? They bought cows, eh? If we had a field—a big, grassy field, I wouldn't mind having a few cows, maybe four or five. We'd have plenty of milk to drink—wouldn't that be nice? I would like to have a big family, and children need to drink lots of milk. Not only that, we could use the cow dung to make natural gas—you know, for fuel, to cook our rice. Besides that, we could breed them, and sell the calves. What do you think, Sida? Hanuman would love cows," he declared on his son's behalf, then paused, and frowned. "What was that remark about 'your pretty little Apson' supposed to mean?"

Sida raised her eyebrows. "Oh, nothing. I suppose I wouldn't mind a cow or two. I could use the fertilizer in the garden."

"If we had a big field, though, what I'd really like to have is horses," Thotsakan continued. "In the evenings, I'd come home and go out riding on my horse—it would be good exercise, don't you think? All the doctors are for exercise nowadays, you know."

She could see that her demon was picturing himself in one of his favorite cowboy movies, riding off on his horse in a cloud of dust. A little boy stands before a house, looking after him miserably and sobbing, *"Chane! Chane! Kham baek, Chane!"*

5. "Apson" (อัปสร) can be used as a female name. It means, "female celestial being."

98

"Who would be getting the exercise?" Sida asked, with the hint of a smile on her lips. "The horse?"

Thotsakan scratched his head.

"They don't give milk," Sida said. "And I'm not so sure you could cook much rice with horse-dung gas. But one thing I am sure of is that nobody eats horse meat these days."

"All right, then we'll stay with cows. Cow dung would work."

Sida pictured her demon mounted on the back of a cow, trundling across the field until he fell off and lay sprawled in the weeds. She smiled in the darkness. Thotsakan saw her smile, and was cheered.

"I see you smiling," he said. "You'd like those cows, wouldn't you?"

Hanuman giggled. "Our mama! That's how she is, chi-i-i-ldren!"

Sida laughed, rose, and lifted her child. Thotsakan stood up, and she set the boy on his father's shoulders, put her arm around her demon's pudgy waist, and the three of them began to walk, partners in dreaming. Sida was only too familiar with Thotsakan's dreams of *apson*—both celestial, and next door. In her own dreams, her winsome young neighbor Apson had been a victim for some time.

And so they all dreamed on, until . . .

Thotsakan and Sida's neighborhood was somewhat remote from the center of town, and might have been lonely and dreary but for a few other houses that had been built around them. The people who lived in these houses they knew by sight or sound; that is, if anyone got drunk and loud, and started cursing someone else's mother, they were likely to know the identity of both the drunk and the mother. They had to listen to the music from the neighbors' tape recorders, and the neighbors had to listen to the music from theirs. Worse, everyone had to listen to the voice of the *kamnan*, over loudspeakers. The *kamnan* was a man who loved his loudspeakers. He also loved his uniform, and carried himself like a man of influence.[6] Twice a day, they heard the national anthem: at 8:00 in the morning, and at 6:00 in the evening. The *kamnan* expected everyone who had not been able to escape his field of vision in time to stand at attention while it was playing. Throughout the day, he graciously provided a steady stream of advice on such matters as the importance of making merit by bringing things for the monks at the local temple, and making merit at the local spirit house of the village, to honor the mother and father spirits.[7] The loudspeaker also was loaned to villagers on special occasions, to broadcast the noise of their party so that no one would feel left out.[8]

6. The *kamnan* (กำนัน) is the leader of a cluster of villages, elected by the village leaders.

7. Most Buddhist Thai households will have a "spirit house"—a relic of pre-Buddhist animism—somewhere on their property. A village may also have its common spirit house, near the edge of the settlement. Spirit houses also may be seen on the grounds of businesses, hotels, and so on. The purpose of this tradition is to show respect for people who have lived (and died) on the property, as well as for the *chao thi*, the major spirit on a specific plot of land. People show respect by placing flowers, candles, joss sticks, and other items at the front of the spirit house.

8. Although these stories are set in an ex-urban Bangkok neighbor-

This afternoon, groups of young men, and some not so young, out of work but not yet out of liquor, milled about enjoying themselves in their way. Suddenly, from somewhere in their midst came the unmistakable sounds of a fight—a fight that would turn out to be no ordinary village scuffle.

"*Ai* Khon has the tiger in him!" a man shouted excitedly. People began running to see what was going on. They could hear the throaty, low roar of a tiger, all right—a low, scary sound something like, "*ho-o-o-k ho-o-o-k hm-m-m-m*" that attracted some people to the furor, and frightened others away. The circle of drinking buddies dispersed to form a wider, safer circle around the tiger-possessed Phaya Khon, who happened to be the elder brother of the fair Apson.[9]

Phaya Khon's bare shoulders and chest bulged with muscles and were covered with dark hair. He was a handsome giant of a lad who could not but remind one of the famous Indian actor Rachender Kuman. He was a bit younger than Thotsakan; all in all, they were quite similar in appearance.

"*Ai* Khon," someone shouted, "are you crazy? These are your friends, here, you crazy bastard! Can't you take a little teasing?"

---

hood that once was a village, in many ways it remains a village.

9. *Phaya* is a title from olden days. In the *Ramakian*, Phaya Khon (พญาขร) is one of Thotsakan's demon retainers. While the narrator of this story refers to him as "Phaya" Khon, the neighbors refer to him as "*Ai* Khon," a far less exalted prefix.

Ai Khon was on all fours now, occasionally giving a fearful leap toward one of the spectators. Indeed, once you knew he was a tiger, he was a very good tiger—although it must be said that he might have been some other animal, had you not known that he was a tiger. A large, angry dog, perhaps.

Another man ran forward bravely, meaning to subdue him, but the strength of *Ai* Khon, Ram the Indian's strange son, now turned tiger, was beyond subduing.

"He is possessed, no doubt of that!" the first man said. "I heard him say that he went and got a tiger tattooed on the crown of his head. So when somebody hits him on the head, this is what happens."

At that moment Ram the Indian stepped forward, hitched up his sarong, and grabbed a fistful of his son's hair.

"Drunk again, you little shit!" Ram the Indian continued to curse his son as the two of them toppled into a dried-up ditch, pummeling each other all the way.[10]

People have two motives in gathering to watch such events: the first is to have a bit of scandal to share, the second to cheer on the participants. Surrounded as he was by noisy onlookers, Phaya Khon managed to lash out in every direction without letting go of his father and then,

10. Ram the Indian's curse is translated in equivalent English cursing. In the Thai text, Ram calls his son *"ai hia"* (ไอ้เหี้ย). A *hia* is a water monitor, a large lizard whose name amounts to a very obscene and completely untranslatable curse. This word is so objectionable that it is printed in the Thai story as เห—, exactly as English-language newspapers continue to represent "four letter words" such as "f—" and "sh—."

in one final, tremendous feat, he managed to hurl him into the air, and send him flying a considerable distance. But he was soon on his feet, and grappling with his son.

"*Pri-ang! Pri-ang! Si-ang fa faaat!*" the crowd cheered, in the words of the popular song, clapping their hands together loudly in time to the words.[11]

"*Ho-o-o-k ho-o-o-k h-m-m-m!*" roared the tiger-possessed Khon, for now he had received blows on the head in earnest!

The battle between the father and the son was a mighty one. They had made a wide circle of trampled grass and mashed dog turds; their onlookers had to scatter and re-group every few moments. One man dashed forward bravely to grab a small, flat whiskey bottle that lay on the ground.

Hanuman stood between his parents, clutching their hands tightly. Sida could see her demon's mouth twitching with words he finally could not contain. "If I were his older brother, I'd teach him a thing or two—the shame of it, wrestling his own father into the dirt!"

Sida urged her husband toward home, dreading the possibility that he would decide it was his duty to interfere

11. These words constitute the refrain of an infamous song of the 1970s. Their meaning is, "Crash! Crash! The thunder sounds!" The song from which they are taken, *Nak phaendin* (หนักแผ่นดิน) was popularized after the 1976 coup d'etat that restored military rule after three years of an open political process, and ushered in a repressive era during which many pro-democracy figures fled the country, or were imprisoned. The author gives the refrain of this song to the crowd surrounding the fight to identify them (and those who had destroyed the pro-democracy movement) as an ignorant, bloodthirsty mob.

in his neighbor's problems. Hanuman trailed along behind them. "Drunks! That's how they are, chi-i-i-ldren!" he pronounced; which, as far as Sida was concerned, summed up the situation pretty well.

Gok-gok! Someone was knocking at the door. "Khun Thotsakan, please open up!"

The sun had set. Thotsakan and Sida were watching election return from the Philippines, and Hanuman was practicing tiger leaps.[12] The kite winds were changing direction, and Thotsakan began muttering angrily, for the smell of Ram the Indian's new cows was now blowing toward them.

It was Ram the Indian himself. "Khun Thotsakan, come and see our *Ai* Khon, please! I have no idea what to do with him! He returned to our house, but when I tried only to talk to him, the bastard started his fits all over again. He has thrown things all over and caused a mess, sir—I don't know what to do, and that's the truth!"

The four of them set off. Hanuman could barely contain his excitement, for he was sure to learn some new tiger tricks, some new poses that would display his *kamlang phainai!*[13]

12. This story was written in 1986, not long after Corazon Aquino came to power in the Philippines. The months leading up to her victory were of particular interest to politically minded Thais, who considered the Ferdinand Marcos administration similar to the military regime that they had overthrown—at least, for three years (1973–76).

13. *Kamlang phainai*/กำลังภายใน means "strength within." In popular culture, it is the property of superheroes such as Ultraman or Superman.

Some of members of the afternoon's cheering crowd were there, but now they looked worried, and whispered together as they looked fearfully toward the door behind which Phaya Khon had secluded himself.

Sida was well aware that Thotsakan's demeanor had changed, as they walked to the neighbor's house. No longer was he Thotsakan the dreamer; he had become Thotsakan the demon of reason and action—qualities which, in fact, endeared him to Sida, and made her proud to be his wife.

"Perhaps he has suffered some disappointment in love," Thotsakan said gravely, addressing the other family members, "and his heart is broken. Or perhaps he is ill. If I were you, I would leave him in there for a day or two, and he will probably come out on his own."

But the family of Ram the Indian did not agree.

"Not at all, sir. His friends invited him to go for this stupid tattoo on the head, and here you see it—he is quite possessed."

This family, thought Thotsakan, worshiped the god Nara-yan. Was it possible that the god had decided to reincarnate himself as a tiger, in *Ai* Khon? Now that was a fearful possibility . . .

"It is said," continued Ram the Indian, "that in order to correct such a thing, one must sharply flick the ear of the one who is affected, and the spirit will depart at once. But who is brave enough to do this, I ask you? Moreover, should anyone go into that room with a mind to flicking his ear, my son would suspect at once."

A little, worried-looking Thai woman stepped forward. She was *Ai* Khon's mother. "I'm just afraid that my boy is going to be sick from all this," she whined, wringing her hands uselessly.

Thotsakan gave a low chuckle. Like the rest of them, the woman had no ideas, only fears. "Perhaps we should go in together," he said to Ram the Indian. He was beginning to feel a curious eagerness to test himself, to prove once and for all who was the stronger . . . Hm-m-m . . . Would the fellow have the courage to come up against the might of Thotsakan? "Why," he thought to himself, "I haven't a doubt that I could wrap this fellow up with— well, with the strength of one of those Sea Games fellows, and—and then some."[14]

Studying his face, Sida suspected deep in her heart that what her demon most desired was a chance to show off in front of Apson.

"I don't want you to go in there," she said. "You might hurt yourself for nothing. Let me talk to him. After all, the tiger isn't likely to do anything to a woman."

"Oh, no, sister!" Apson cried out, sounding shocked. "You don't understand. My brother isn't himself—you mustn't go in there. Leave it to the men!"

Thotsakan beamed at Apson. "Look at her," he thought. "Isn't she adorable? Even troubling to worry herself about Sida. Such behavior surely bodes well for future possibilities; what splendid good fortune may yet be mine."[15]

14. Asian Games, which had just ended, in Thailand.
15. Much is implied. The author suggests that Thotsakan is seeing

Leave it to the men? Sida picked up Hanuman, handed him to Apson, strode across the room and knocked firmly on *Ai* Khon's bedroom door. Then she turned to the astonished crowd, putting her finger to her lips. Silence, please. She turned the knob and entered the room, leaving the door open—as open as the mouth of the demon general, who stood gaping, his eyes bulging out.

"Nothing soft about you," Thotsakan muttered when they had returned home. "As brave as an army of men with chests the span of three *sok*, that's my wife![16] Hrr-r . . . so the great Phaya Khon is defeated by a woman! Yet, you must forgive me for asking why you had to interfere in something that was none of your business. I am curious."

The lovely Sida was not the least angered by her demon's sarcastic tone, and smiled cheerfully at him in the darkness. "If no one got hurt, wasn't it for the best? And I had nothing to worry about, since, if worse came to worse for me, there was someone who would be delighted to look after my son. And my husband."

Thotsakan tried to suppress a grin by baring his demonic fangs, but it was to no avail. "All right, tell me— how did you get close enough to *Ai* Khon to flick his ear?"

Apson's apparently solicitous behavior toward Sida as an excellent indicator of the future harmony of his household, should Apson join it as a "minor wife." The author also suggests that this is but another "Thotsakan dream," and that Sida would surely squash any such attempt on the part of either Apson or Thotsakan.

16. The *sok* (ศอก) is a traditional Thai measurement, from elbow to fingertip—in modern times, one cubit or fifty centimeters.

Sida burst into laughter. "Flick his ear? If I had tried to do such a thing, the tiger might have bitten me. I simply asked him what was wrong. Did his head hurt? Did he have a fever? And then we talked, about nothing in particular. He spoke quite normally, and I didn't see any 'tiger,' I assure you. Which reminds me . . . Did you believe that *Ai* Khon was possessed by a tiger spirit?"

"What difference does it make? The thing is—the thing is that I didn't like you going in there with him. I don't want you to have anything to do with—with anybody, do you understand?"

CHAPTER FOUR

Humor, Myth, and the Prophetic Pen

THE USES OF HUMOR

It is typical of women's rewriting of myth that, when meanings already latent in a given story are recovered and foregrounded by a woman's perspective, the entire story appears to change . . . [The] feature of feminist revisionism which scholars find most irritating and which I consider essential to the work of feminism [is that] the feminist [writer] replays tragedy as farce. (Ostriker 1993: 29)

[Sida] could see that her demon was picturing himself in one of his favorite cowboy movies, riding off on his horse in a cloud of dust. A little boy stands before a house, looking after him miserably and sobbing, *"Chane! Chane! Kham baek, Chane!"* ("Phaya Khon Possessed," 75)

In her use of humor, Sri Daoruang parts company with many Thai writers who represent the "literature of social consciousness."[1] By and large, they are vigilant about keeping a straight face out of respect for the seriousness of their cause.[2] But Sri Daoruang is fascinated by the vanities and foibles of human beings and particularly relishes the ridiculous aspects of the human condition. In her *Ramakian*-based parodies, "Lanka"/Thailand is ruled by men who are less evil than they are vain, corrupt, and foolish:

> The *kamnan* [district officer] was a man who loved his loudspeakers. He also loved his uniform, and carried himself like a man of influence. Twice a day, they heard the national anthem: at 8:00 in the morning, and at 6:00 in the evening. The *kamnan* expected everyone who had not been able to escape his field of vision in time to stand at attention while it was playing. Throughout the day, he graciously provided a steady stream of advice . . . ("Phaya Khon Possessed," 76)

Another example of the advantages Sri Daoruang realizes through the use of humor is her revenge upon the

---

1. For information on Thailand's "literature of social conscious-ness" see works by Phillips, Anderson, and Harrison, in the bibliography.

2. The great exception is Phaibun Wongthet's hilarious work, *Chan chueng ma ha khwam ngoi* (ฉันจึงมาหาความหงอย), a collection of essays parodying his fellow political activists. This was written in exile, in Sweden, following the military crackdown of 1976. See Kepner 2001.

"*E* Monthos" of modern Thai society, in the story "Sida Puts Out the Fire," when Sida comes across evidence that Thotsakan may be having an affair.

> Sida was sure that [*E* Montho] must be beautiful—in the way women who worked out in the world were beautiful. In fact, she was probably—oh, no! She was probably— an intellectual! ("Sida Puts Out the Fire," 66)

Sida imagines *E* Montho working "out in the world"— but not in a factory, or as another woman's servant. She is an intellectual, and has a profession—perhaps the profession of writing, as practiced not by a housewife writer, but by writers with a university education. The *E* Monthos of the Thai world sit on committee, bestow awards and approbation upon those they deem worthy, and are treated with respect by their peers, and with deference by their inferiors.

Sida eventually triumphs—not over *E* Montho, but over the jealousy and envy in her own heart. In the end, *E* Montho simply doesn't matter very much.

By using characters from the *Ramakian*, Sri Daoruang is able to play with the pieces on the chess board of Thai society to her heart's delight. For example, the carpenter who builds Thotsakan's library, in the story "Thotsakan Puts Down the *Chingchoks*" is called "Nai Ong-In"; he is named after the god In(dra), who has an important role in the original tale. Why, I wondered while translating this story, had the author transformed the god Indra into a carpenter in an ex-urban Bangkok neighborhood? I was also puzzled by the character of Benchakai, the neighborhood girl whose flagrant ineptitude as a baby-sitter is described in "Thotsakan to the Garden" (56). She is named after a character in the *Ramakian* who is the niece of Thotsakan, best known for her (unwilling) portrayal of Sida in a failed plot to convince Prince Ram that she is already dead, so that he will give up trying to find her. Again, I searched in vain for clues that would tie Sri Daoruang's Benchakai to the one in the original tale.

Finally, I wrote to the author, apologizing for my lack of acuity in this matter. She promptly replied that except for Sida, Thotsakan, and Hanuman, and the "Ramalaks," there was no relationship between the minor characters in her stories and their namesakes in the *Ramakian*: she had used their names for her minor characters because "I just thought it would be funny to make 'high' characters in the original stories 'low' in my stories." "Moreover," she added, "If I had had time, I would have included the name of every character in the *Ramakian*."

THE RE-VISION OF HANUMAN

The shock and terror that Sri Daoruang and her husband Suchat experienced as the result of their own son's birth with heart malformations, and the relentless battle, year after precious year, to keep him alive, explain the choice of Hanuman as the child of Thotsakan and Sida in the demon folk tales. Hanuman is very much like "Tanu," the frail little boy who is the subject of the painful, autobiographical short story mentioned in chapter 1.[3]

> During the first year of Tanu's life, his doctor . . . said that it was important for us to raise Tanu like any ordinary child, so that, if he did grow to adulthood, he would not have an inferiority complex. Then he told us that we should not allow Tanu to become tired, and that we must try to prevent his catching colds . . . Tanu perspires a great deal. At night his pillow becomes soaked, and his mattress . . . I wipe his tender skin with a soft cloth . . . I buy the softest, lightest clothing I can for him, but even so, sometimes he refuses to sleep with a shirt on, and when he gets a cold, he perspires more, and if I do not keep his head dry, blisters cover his forehead.
>
> And yet, who does not know that Tanu is the star of our hearts? We are exactly like other parents. He was the cutest little baby in the world, and now he is the cutest little boy. It is what I think, although I know what other people see . . . A small, homely boy whose head is too large, whose ears stick out, and who is very thin . . . They don't notice the clear, sparkling round eyes; the beautiful long eyelashes; the *clean, white little teeth*.[4]

As everyone knows who has seen his antics in the *like*, Hanuman, the "pale little monkey" of the *Ramakian*, is an

---

3. Sri Daoruang's son, Mon Sawatsri, is now a healthy adult, a writer like his parents and also an artist.

4. From my English translation of Tanu," unpublished as of this writing.

agile fellow indeed, not only full of fun but, most important of all, invincible, fearless, and indestructible.

> Little baby Hanuman . . . saw the glorious Sun rise into the air like a big ripe mango fruit. New born though he was, he knew what fruit was. He licked his *sharp bright little teeth*, crouched down and jumped with a leap and a bound up into the sky and went flying straight at the Sun. (Buck 1986: 187, italics added)

Regardless of what befalls him, nothing can destroy the Hanuman of the *Ramakian*. The following passage is from the 1967 Chalermnit Press volume entitled *The Ramayana* (no author or translator noted):

> All kinds of methods were used in order to kill Hanuman, but he always escaped unkilled and sat laughing. Then Ravana brought out a musth (sic) and fierce elephant to stamp him to death, but Hanuman escaped from the fetters and feet of the elephant, climbed up on its back, killed the mahout, and broke the elephant's neck. Ravana did not know how to kill him, then Hanuman told him that he was invulnerable to all methods of killing except by fire. Ravana . . . ordered cotton soaked with oil to be wound round . . . Hanuman and set fire to it . . . Hanuman with fire burning all over his body ran about the palace setting fire to every room . . . Very soon the whole city was aflame. Men and women giants with their children ran about in panic . . . Hanuman now

threw the fire from his body . . . (*Ramayana*, Chalermnit 1967: 52)

In the first story of the series, "Thotsakan and Sida," Hanuman is presented as an evidently robust teenager who is capable of working with his mother, and running errands. But then, the author seemed to have changed her mind, and in all of the subsequent stories she has made him younger, a robust and knockabout little boy.

At his papa's words, he came tumbling onto the scene like an actor in a Chinese movie, landing between his parents in the attitude of a Ninja set to strike. Sida got up and left the jokesters to their tricks. Those two! ("Sida Puts Out the Fire," 63)

In creating the character of Hanuman, Sri Daoruang departs from her principle task in the demon folk tales, which is to use myth and humor in order reveal some truths about contemporary marriage and family life. The Hanuman of these tales is crafted skillfully into a re-vision of experience—not life as it really is, but as it should have been, and ought to be.

CHOOSING THOTSAKAN

Perhaps the first decision Sri Daoruang made in writing the first story, "Thotsakan and Sida," was to recast Princess Sida as Everywoman. This was not terribly difficult, for even in the original tale, Sida is given quite human dimen-sions. After suffering Ram's jealousy and suspicion, after he has banished her and then ordered her death, she suffers the ultimate insult to her pride, returning to her husband at the urging of the gods. Before the final reconciliation, Ram himself entreats Sida to return to his capital. Her only answer is to scornfully berate him for the years during which she has suffered his jealousy, suspicion, and cruelty.

> The longer Sida listened [to Prince Ram], the more her bitterness increased. "Do not come to me with your sweet words, and think that I will hear them, and believe you. When [Thotsakan] took me away to his demon land, I lived outside his palace walls, in a garden filled with guards; you sent Hanuman, to discover whether [I had kept my virtue]; and when I returned to you celestial ladies also bore witness [that I had]. For all that, your suspicion never ceased. And now, I live alone, gathering fruit to sustain myself in this wild wood. For ten years there has been no one to watch over me in this place where hunters roam, and holy men and sorcerers. Why, you should suspect me now far more than you ever did while I lived in Lanka. You are a great leader, with a palace full of concubines; and I am nothing but a wicked woman, with whom you should not think to sully your honor."
> (Premseri Thai prose version of the *Ramakian*, 1977: 596)

Following this exchange, Ram, realizing that he has no chance of shaking Sida's resolve to remain alone in her "wild wood" by virtue of either his charm or his unconvincing apologies (which consist mainly of blaming the "fate" which led him to order her death by his brother's hand), abruptly changes his approach.

> Ram saw that he must take her children back with him, and leave her there alone in the woods to become lonely. Because no woman in the world could cease to love her children; and, longing for them, Sida would surely get over her pique. After he had kept them awhile, he would invite her, and she would come at once. (Premsiri 1977: 597)

When he tells her that he will take his children to the capital, Sida replies:

> "My beloved children are not your offspring. Look carefully at them, and you will see how like Thotsakan they are. Why take them with you? We are all evil, you see, the mother and the children too . . . Why take them, when with your next fit of temper you may order their death?" (Premsiri 1977: 597)

Ram, after another pretty speech in which he begs Sida not to be so unduly harsh, breaks down into sobs. But she is unmoved: "The more he wept, the angrier she became . . . " (Premsiri 1977: 597)

Sida may be all that is loyal, virtuous, and "good," but she has her limits, and she certainly has her pride. Sri Daoruang has chosen to give this woman, in her contemporary incarnation, another fate, and another mate: not the pious prince, but the difficult demon.

In the *Ramakian*, when Thotsakan hears (false) rumors that his son Intarachit has defeated both Prince Ram and his brother Prince Lak, we are told that he "laugh[s] with his ten merry mouths, clapping loudly with his twenty hands . . ." Later, when he learns the bitter truth, and looks upon his son's corpse, "with all ten mouths, Thotsakan lament[s], and wail[s] his grief." (Srisurang and Sumalaya 1982: 47)

It would be difficult to find a more illustrative contrast between the character of Prince Ram, and the character of Thotsakan the demon king, than these two images: Ram weeping before Sida in the hope of winning back her affections, while inwardly plotting to force her return by taking her children; and Thotsakan, mindlessly wailing in grief over the body of his son Intarachit—albeit he has caused that death himself through his mad campaign to possess Sida. Thotsakan is all impulse and emotion, and his desires lead inevitably to disaster, in both the original *Ramakian* and in Sri Daoruang's stories. Ram and Lak, in the original *Ramakian*, are winners in the eyes of the world, brothers who achieve glory despite all. In the contemporary tales, Sri Daoruang relegates them to the ignominious role of "the Ramalaks of the marketplace," shallow and greedy "establishment" figures against whom her dear demon "would continue to go into battle . . . again and again, all by himself." ("Thotsakan and Sida," 29)

The Thotsakan of myth fights with daggers clutched in twenty mighty fists; the Thotsakan Sri Daoruang gives us chases tiny lizards with a fly swatter. If the mythical Thotsakan had eighty-four thousand wives, the contemporary Thotsakan has as many dreams, with which he insists upon regaling his wife. Indeed, dreams are a mainstay in the relationship of this couple, whose budget does not support many other amusements.

Although he muses about "celestial ladies" and other females who, he assures her, would understand him better than Sida does, he is quite aware of the truth: that Sida not only understands him perfectly, but knows him better than he knows himself. And, he knows that she knows . . . They understand each other very well.

> "Sida, a woman who truly understands me, who truly loves me—let us say that one or two such women came to live with us. Would you mind? Of course, I would choose women less beautiful than you."
>
> Sida was used to this kind of teasing from her demon general. He talked a lot, but she had yet to see any of these women appear. ("Thotsakan: Sick of War," 55)

> . . .Thotsakan and Sida began to speak of one thing and another, of new dreams and old ones. The subjects of their two-track conversation merged at points, and diverged at others. They expressed both reasonable thoughts and seemingly senseless ones, and various combinations of both; in short, it was the sort of conversation two people often have when they are alone together, and have been married for a long time. (57–58)

Sida may grow frustrated with Thotsakan, tired of his teasing, exasperated by his stubbornness—but she is sometimes overwhelmed by his tenderness, and touched by his thoughtful, clumsy gestures. Despite his modest earnings, Thotsakan likes to think of himself as the "'shade of the po tree, shade of the banyan tree,' under which his little family [is] able to live a contented and happy life." ("Thotsakan and Sida," 27) He is deeply wounded by Sida's decision to supplement the family income by going to work.

In the *Ramakian*, Thotsakan is infamous for his sexual appetites and lack of emotional restraint; but he is also known for his credulity, and a certain "innocence" that seems greatly at odds with his fabled ferocity. Sri Dao-ruang's Thotsakan shares this credulity, this innocence; what he lacks is not intelligence, but a certain knowledge of the world that cannot be achieved through his beloved books. In order to improve his family's standard of living, he opens his door to "the Ramalaks of the marketplace." They walk in, eagerly, and they offer him—credit.

> Here it is, look! A color television set—see? A fourteen-inch screen! And there—look! A gas stove with four burners, and an oven besides. These were the machines that supplied convenience, and also modern happiness . . . ("Thotsakan and Sida," 29)

Sida, unable or unwilling to think of herself as changed from the "up-country factory worker" she once was, is attracted to and comfortable with a male who also is marginalized in society, not because he used to work in a factory, or clean houses for rich people, but because he seems unable—or unwilling—to achieve worldly success in a society that worships it. His ideals, which he will never abandon, ensure that he will never enjoy social or economic parity with the "Ramalaks" of modern Thailand.

At the time the tales of the demon folk were written, Sri Daoruang's husband, Suchat, was a rather discouraged middle-aged man who had lived through momentous, heart-breaking battles against the "Ramalaks" of the Thai establishment—not only economic but political and military "Ramalaks" as well. Such men did not hesitate to order the massacre of unarmed students and other people protesting corrupt military rule. But as the years went by, and especially during the prosperous 1980s and 1990s—until the economic crash of 1997—many Thais forgot what the battles had been all about. Suchat never forgot, and has remained uncompromising and true to his ideals. Clearly, he means to fight on against the Ramalaks, forever.

This is a man who, for all of his frailties, faults, and failed dreams, his teasing and his tantrums, she can understand and love—and, in the end, respect—with all her heart.

SRI DAORUANG AND THE PROPHETIC PEN

Quite a few Thai women identify themselves as at least sympathetic to feminism, which generally is equated with the pursuit of economic and social parity. There also is a Buddhist feminist movement, the major objective of which is a greater role for women in Buddhist practice, which remains focused upon monks and temples. A small percentage of Buddhist women support the idea of women's ordination. Women may become Buddhist nuns, but they cannot be ordained and achieve a status equal to that of the highly respected male monks.[5]

Despite the activities of a few dedicated women, I suspect that it will be the "prophetic pen" of contemporary women writers like Sri Daoruang, interpreting and conveying the conditions of women's lives, and defining the character and the dimensions of their aspirations, that will prove most important to the progress of the feminist movement in Thailand. That Sri Daoruang already holds such a prophetic pen in her hand is suggested by the fact that she already has run afoul of the Thai establishment (literary, academic, social, and political). The complaint is that she simply goes "too far . . ."

In many of the short stories she has written before and after "The Tales of the Demon Folk," Sri Daoruang plainly reveals the less admirable aspects of Thai society, revealing injustice, unfairness, discrimination, and hypocrisy. Sometimes, she even goes so far as to cast popular Thai Buddhist beliefs in a not altogether favorable light. This is almost unheard of. Her critics have struck back with two main charges: First, that she is not capable of addressing social issues, because of her limited education, and ought not to try. (For example, a Thai professor of literature told me, "These *Ramakian* stories don't work, you see. *She goes too far, and anyway, she hasn't the back-*

5. See Kepner 1996, 33–39; and Chatsumarn 1991.

ground to do this sort of thing . . .") A second major charge
is that she shows a lack of respect for Thai culture, choos-
ing to focus on ugly subjects that do not need to be ex-
posed in fiction.

"Ugly subjects" certainly dominate "Have You Seen My
Dog?" a short story about a little boy who has been
abandoned by his mother in a slum, and wanders about all
day, alone.[6] At the end of the story, neighbors realize that
the child has eaten his own dog. In another short story,
"Mating Snakes," a woman is fascinated by two snakes
copulating in a mud puddle in the lane outside her house.
But the controversy over "ugly" stories was nothing com-
pared to the charges of blasphemy following the publication of the short story "Matsi," the title of which refers to
a revered character in one of the Buddhist tales that are
called "jatakas": tales of the previous lives of the Buddha,
before he was finally born as Prince Siddhartha, achieved
enlightenment, and became the Buddha.[7] Most conserva-
tive Buddhists regard any popular treatment of any of the
jataka stories as tasteless at best, and blasphemous at
worst.[8] Despite the controversy over the short story, a
collection of stories that contained the offending story,
and in fact was entitled *Matsi*, was nominated for the

6. This story has not been translated into English.
7. Anyone may achieve "buddhahood," or become "a buddha."
Only Prince Siddhartha, after his enlightenment, is known as "the
Buddha."
8. Once a year, a senior monk reads this entire jataka over the radio;
many Thai Buddhists believe that anyone who listens to the entire
presentation (which is called "Mahachat") gain merit by doing so.

SEAWrite award in the early 1990s. Most of the judges agreed that the stories were well written. However, the title story made it impossible to grant the award to this book.[9]

What was so offensive about this story, to so many people? "Matsi" is the wife of Phra Wetsandon, the major character in the last of the jataka tales. In the tale, Phra Wetsandon's faithful wife, Matsi, makes no complaint when he gives their children away to a hermit. He is greatly admired for this act, which proves him to be truly unencumbered by worldly attachments and desires. Matsi, too, is greatly admired for her loyalty to her husband, and her respect for his quest.

The "Matsi" of Sri Daoruang's short story is a desperate, exhausted, nineteen-year-old woman who has been arrested for abandoning her children at a bus stop—after herself being abandoned by their father. "What kind of a person are you?" a frustrated police officer asks her, "To abandon your own children!" The young woman (who is "named" only by the suggestive title "Matsi," but never called by this name or any other, in the story) says that she just wants to give away her children, and go live at a temple. Her happiest memories are of going to the temple with her mother when she was a child. The police officer

9. It is not unusual for the SEAWrite panel of judges to nominate a work that they feel is exceptional, even though they realize that they would be soundly criticized for awarding it the prize. In the past, the SEAWrite award winning book in each year has been printed and distributed to high school students. This has had a predictable effect on the selection of the winning book.

asks her what she would do there. She would meditate, she says. "You can't just go meditate at a temple, and leave your children," the police officer says contemptuously. "Why not?" she snaps back. "Phra Wetsandon did it, didn't he?" (Sri Daoruang, "Matsi," in *Matsi*, 79–85)[10]

This response so shocks the police officer that he immediately has the young woman taken off to a mental hospital.

Sida, in the tales of the demon folk, is not at all like the young woman in the story "Matsi." She is no one's victim. If Sida is satisfied with her life, for the most part, like the author who created her she also is a great dreamer. Sri Daoruang's fascination with dreaming, and its role in a writer's life, is an important element in a short story she wrote shortly after the death of the beloved writer Suwanee Sukhontha. It is in the form of a letter to Suwanee.

> You [Suwanee] used to say that one reason writing is hard is that one is mired in lavish private dreams, dreaming within oneself these stories and words, words, words . . . Yes, we are dreaming all the time, and there is no end of it until there is an end of us.[11]

10. My English translation of this short story appears in Kepner 1996.

11. From Sri Daoruang's short story, "The Letter You Never Received." My translation. See Kepner 1995.

In each of the tales of the demon folk, Sida dreams—never aloud, but to herself. She dreams of a future that she hopes will be more fulfilling, and more satisfying in some respects than her life is at present. But in her dreams, she is never a woman alone.

"Sida stared at her husband. Wasn't he wonderful? She felt laughter in her heart . . ." ("Phaya Khon Possessed," 81)

There will always be someone standing beside Sida, when she dreams of the future. Come what may, she will still be married to the demon king.

Bibliography

Works in English

Anderson, Benedict, and Ruchira Mendiones. *In the Mirror: Literature and Politics in Siam in the American Era*. Bangkok: Duang Kamol, 1985.

Bofman, Theodora Helene. *The Poetics of the Ramakian*. DeKalb, IL: Northern Illinois University Center for Southeast Asian Studies. Monograph Series on Southeast Asia, 1984.

Botan. *Letters from Thailand*. Translated by Susan F. Kepner. Chiang Mai, Thailand: Silkworm Books, 2002.

Cadet, J. M. *The Ramakien: The Stone Rubbings of the Thai Epic*. 2nd ed. Tokyo: Kodansha International Ltd., 1975.

Chart Kobjitti. *The Judgment*. Translated by Laurie Maund. Bangkok: Laurie Maund, 1983.

Chatsumarn Kabilsingh. *Thai Women in Buddhism*. Berkeley: Parallax Press, 1991.

Chetana Nagavajara "Parody as Translation: A Thai Case Study [of parodies by Phaibun Wongthed]." In *Comparative Literature from a Thai Perspective*. Chulalongkorn University Press, 1996.

———. "Unsex Me Here: An Oriental's Plea for Gender Reconciliation." *Silpakorn University Journal* (September 1992–February 1993): 251–268.

Dhammapada. Translated by Irving Babbitt. New York: A New Directions Paperback by Oxford University Press, 1965.

Gross, Rita M. *Buddhism After Patriarchy: A Feminist History, Analysis, and Reconstruction of Buddhism.* Albany: State University of New York Press, 1993.

Harrison, Rachel. *A Drop of Glass and Other Stories.* Bangkok: Duang Kamol, 1985. [Collected translations of fiction by Sri Daoruang.]

Kepner, Susan F. "A Massacre of Meanings: Phaibun Wongthet's 'And So I Come in Search of Fed-up-ness.'" Paper presented at the Conference on Violence in Southeast Asia, University of California, Berkeley, February 2001.

————. *The Lioness in Bloom: Modern Thai Fiction about Women.* Berkeley: University of California Press, 1996.

————. "The Letter You Never Received," translation of a short story by Sri Dao Ruang. In *Two Lines/Tracks,* Olivia Sears, ed. Stanford University, Spring 1995.

Mills, Mary Beth. "Modernity and Gender Vulnerability: Rural Women Working in Bangkok." In *Gender and Development in Southeast Asia,* pp. 83–89. Edited by Penny and John Van Esterik. Proceedings of the Twentieth Meeting of the Canadian Council for Southeast Asian Studies, York University, October 18–20, 1991. (Available from CASA Secretariat, McFill University, 3434 McTavish Street, Montreal, QC H3A 1X9 Canada.)

Morell, David, and Chai-anan Samudavanija. *Political Conflict in Thailand: Reform, Reaction, Revolution.* Cambridge: Oelgeschlager, Gunn & Hain, Publishers, Inc., 1982.

The National Identity Board (of Thailand). *Women in Thai Literature (Book One).* Bangkok: Office of the Prime Minister, 1992.

Nitaya Masavisut. "Kindling the Literary Flame." Paper delivered at the Fifth International Conference on Thai Studies, School of Oriental and African Studies, University of London, July 1993.

Ostriker, Alicia Suskin. *Feminist Revision and the Bible.* Cambridge: Blackwell Publishers, 1993.

————. "The Theory Debate: Both Sides Now." *The Cream City Review* 15.2 (Fall 1991): 37–41.

Pailin Rungrat. Letter to the author, 1991.

Phillips, Herbert P. *Modern Thai Literature: An Ethnographic Interpretation*. Honolulu: University of Hawaii Press, 1987.

Puri, Swami Satyananda, and Charoen Sarahiran. *The Ramakirti (Ramakien) or The Thai Version of The Ramayana*. Bangkok: Thai-Bharat Cultural Lodge and Satyananda Puri Foundation, 1949.

Raghavan, V., ed. *The Ramayana Tradition in Asia*. New Delhi: Sahitya Akademi, 1980.

Rahula, Walpole. *What the Buddha Taught*. New York: Grove Weidenfeld, 1974.

Rama I, King Phutthaloetlanaphalai. *Ramayana* (Complete title: *Ramayana Masterpiece of Thai Literature retold from the original version by King Rama I of Siam*) 2nd ed. Printed by Chalermnit Press, distributed by Chalermnit Bookshop, 1967.

"Rambo and Rama." *The Economist*. 20 Feb.1988: 97.

Reynolds, Craig, ed. *National Identity and Its Defenders: Thailand 1939–1989*. Chiang Mai, Thailand: Silkworm Books, 1991. Rev. ed 2002.

Ruenruthai Sujjapun. "Female Characters in Narrative Poetry." Paper delivered at the Fifth International Conference on Thai Studies, School of Oriental and African Languages, London, 1993.

Shastri, Satya Vrat. *Sriramakirtimahakavyam (A Sanskrit Mahakavya on the Thai Ramakien)*. Bangkok: Moolamall Sachdev Foundation and Amarnath Sachdeva Foundation, 1990.

Siburapha. *Behind the Painting and Other Stories*. Translated and edited by David Smyth, with an introduction. Singapore: Oxford University Press, 1990.

Sidaoru'ang [Sri Daoruang]. *A Drop of Glass and Other Stories*. Translated and with an introducton by Rachel Harrison. Bangkok: Duang Kamol, 1994.

Somporn Varnado Wattanasan. "Social and Cultural Constraints on Modern Thai Women." Paper delivered at the Conference on Gender and Culture in Literature and Film, East and West: Issues of Perception and Interpretation. Chiang Mai, 1992. (A joint venture of Chiang Mai University, Chulalongkorn University, the

Institute of Culture and Communication of the East-West Center, Honolulu, Hawaii; and the College of Languages, Linguistics and Literature, University of Hawaii, Honolulu, HI.)

Spivak, Gayatri Chakravorty. *In Other Worlds: Essays in Cultural Politics.* Routledge-Routledge, Chapman, & Hall, Inc., 1988.

Stimpson, Catharine R. "Feminist Criticism." In *Redrawing the Boundaries: The Transformation of English and American Literary Studies,* pp. 251–269. Edited by Stephen Greenblatt and Giles Gunn. New York: The Modern Language Association of America, 1992.

Sutherland, Sally J. "Sita and Draupadi: Aggressive Behavior and Female Role-Models in the Sanskrit Epics." *Journal of the American Oriental Society* 109.1 (1989): 63–78.

Suvanna Kriengkraipetch, and Smith, Larry E. *Value Conflicts in Thai Society: Agonies of Change Seen in Short Stories.* Bangkok: Social Research Institute, Chulalongkorn University, 1992.

Suwanee Sukhontha. "On a Cloudy Morning." Translated by Susan F. Kepner. In *Tenggaru.* Kuala Lumpur, 1992.

Trisilpa Boonkhachorn, "The Unfinished Pagoda: An Epistemological Perspective on the Theory of Intertextuality." In *Ruam bot an priap thiap* (Collected articles on comparative literature, a volume of essays in Thai and English. (The Trisilpa essay is in English.) Bangkok: Chulalongkorn University Press, 1993.

Wibha Senanan. *The Genesis of the Novel in Thailand.* Bangkok: Thai Watana Panich Co., Ltd., 1975.

Wyatt, David. *Thailand: A Short History.* New Haven and London: Yale University Press, 1984. 2nd ed. 2003.

Works in Thai

Note: Authors' given (first) name appears first, according to Thai usage. If an author's preferred spelling of his or her name is known, that spelling is used.

Botan. *Phuying khon nan chue Bunrod*/ผู้หญิงคนนั้นชื่อบุญรอด (That woman's name is Boonrawd). Bangkok: Chomromdek, 1981.

Chinda Ngamsutthi. *Chue nan chandai, lem 1*/ชื่อนั้นฉันใด (Who is the person/character with that name? vol. 1.) Bangkok: Odeon Store, 1990.

Chusak Patarakulwanich. *Khon kap nangsue*/คนกับหนังสือ (People and books) Bangkok: Sarakodi Press, 1993.

Comparative Literature Department, Chulalongkorn University. *Wanakhadi priap thiap, ruam bot an*/วรรณคดีเปรียบเทียบรวมบทอ่าน (Comparative Literature: Collected Essays). Bangkok: Chulalongkorn University Press, 1993.

Kawbkul Ingkuthanon. *Wichan wanakam Thai thet*/วิจารณ์วรรณกรรมไทยเทศ (Criticism of Thai and foreign literature) Bangkok: Swaeng Ha, 1989.

Srisurang Poolthupya and Sumalaya Bangloy. *Tua lakhon nai Ramakian*/ตัวละครในรามเกียรติ์ (Characters in the Ramakian). Bangkok: Odeon Store, 1982.

Premseri, ed. *Ramakian*/รามเกียรติ์ (The Ramakian). Bangkok: Borisat Ruamsan, 1977. (A prose version of the *Ramakian.*)

Sri Daoruang. *Lakhon haeng lok*/ละครแห่งโลก (*Lakhon* is a theatrical performance, *haeng lok* means "of the world.") Bangkok: Writer Magazine, 1994.

———. *Mae Salu*/แม่สาลู (Mother Salu). Bangkok: Duang Kamol, 1992.

———. *Matsi*/มัทรี (Matsi). 2nd printing. Bangkok: Love and Live Press, Ltd., third printing 1990.

———. *Phap luang ta*/ภาพลวงตา (Picture that deceives the eye; or, Illusions.) Bangkok: Love and Live Press, Ltd., 2nd printing 1990.

———. *Bat prachachon*/บัตรประชาชน (Identity card.) Bangkok: Met Sai, 1984.

Thanet Wetpada. *Dinso kho khian*/ดินสอขอเขียน (The pencil asks to write). Bangkok: Papyrus Press, n.d. (?1993)

Wan Pen. "*Nai wanni khong Sri Daoruang*"/ในวันนี้ของศรีดาวเรือง (Sri Dao Ruang today). Interview in *Phraew* 14: 335, 265–271, August 1993.